What is Financialization?

T0271107

This book introduces a new and original analytic approach to defining, under-standing, and explaining financialization. It provides a precise and quantifia-ble definition of financialization, disaggregating financialization into its three varieties. These are examined through the lens of financial development, both before and after the Great Recession, providing the most in-depth analysis of the finance-real economy-labor nexus. It provides a historical perspective, looking at financialization as a key dynamic that has shaped real economic structures in terms of both growth and inequality of income over the last four decades in high-income, upper-middle-income, and lower-middle-income countries. The book makes its multidisciplinary content readily accessible to non-economists by providing economics background information, and to economists by providing social-theoretical context. It will be essential read-ing for academics, researchers, analysts, and students of economics, business, finance, sociology, politics, and international relations. It will also serve as a vital resource for policy-makers and bureaucrats in determining, formulating, implementing, and revising policy alternatives to govern the pros and cons of financial development in terms of its effects on real output and income inequality.

Taner Akan is an associate professor of political economy at the Department of Economics at Istanbul University.

Halil İbrahim Gündüz holds a PhD in panel data econometrics.

Routledge Frontiers of Political Economy

For more information about this series, please visit: www.routledge.com/Routledge-Frontiers-of-Political-Economy/book-series/SE0345

What is Financialization?

Taner Akan and
Halil İbrahim Gündüz

Routledge
Taylor & Francis Group

LONDON AND NEW YORK

First published 2024
by Routledge
4 Park Square, Milton Park, Abingdon, Oxon OX14 4RN

and by Routledge
605 Third Avenue, New York, NY 10158

Routledge is an imprint of the Taylor & Francis Group, an informa business

© 2024 Taner Akan and Halil İbrahim Gündüz

British Library Cataloguing-in-Publication Data
A catalogue record for this book is available from the British Library

Library of Congress Cataloging-in-Publication Data
Names: Akan, Taner, author. | Gündüz, Halil İbrahim, author.
Title: What is financialization? / Taner Akan and Halil İbrahim Gündüz.
Description: Abingdon, Oxon ; New York, NY : Routledge, 2024. |
Series: Routledge frontiers of political economy |
Includes bibliographical references and index.
Identifiers: LCCN 2023041364 (print) | LCCN 2023041365 (ebook) |
ISBN 9781032372655 (hardback) | ISBN 9781032372662 (paperback) |
ISBN 9781003336105 (ebook)
Subjects: LCSH: Financialization.
Classification: LCC HG173 .A366 2024 (print) |
LCC HG173 (ebook) | DDC 332--dc23/eng/20230906
LC record available at https://lccn.loc.gov/2023041364
LC ebook record available at https://lccn.loc.gov/2023041365

ISBN: 978-1-032-37265-5 (hbk)
ISBN: 978-1-032-37266-2 (pbk)
ISBN: 978-1-003-33610-5 (ebk)

DOI: 10.4324/9781003336105

Typeset in Times New Roman
by KnowledgeWorks Global Ltd.

Access the Support Material: www.routledge.com/9781032372655

Contents

About the Authors

Taner Akan is an associate professor at Istanbul University's Department of Economics. Previously, he was a visiting scholar at LSE, Max Planck Institute, and King's College London. He investigates the complementary dynamics of macroeconomic, financial, and environmental governance. His papers appeared in leading journals such as Socio-Economic Review, Cities, Applied Energy, Renewable Energy, and Energy. He is the author of "Institutional System Analysis in Political Economy" and "Complementary Roots of Growth and Development".

Halil İbrahim Gündüz currently works at the University of Maastricht in the Department of Quantitative Economics (QE) as a postdoctoral researcher. He studies the quantification of model uncertainty, using bootstrap, analysis of high-dimensional "Big Data" time series, long-run trends in macroeconomic, energy and climatological time series, risk measures for financial series, and the forecasting of macroeconomic and financial time series. He also actively maintains a number of widely used programming languages such as MATLAB, Python, R, C++, STATA, GAUSS, EViews, SPSS, SAS, RATS, and JMulTi.

Introduction

The debate on financialization revolves around four major themes. First, heterodox political economists focus predominantly on advanced economies, arguing that (i) real economic activity serves the finance sector but not vice versa, the specific illustration of which is the accrual and distribution of profits through the finance sector but not through the real sector (Krippner, 2005), and (ii) that this socially embedded process worsens income inequality (Van der Zwan, 2014). Second, quantitative economists concentrate on the finance-growth nexus, not using the term *financialization* but arguing that the finance sector positively affects growth until its size reaches roughly 100 percent of the gross domestic product (GDP), at which threshold its effect turns negative, illustrating the hypothesis of the U-shaped finance-growth nexus (Arcand et al., 2015; Law & Singh, 2014; Shen & Lee, 2006). The third theme is whether the process of financialization has incurred any change during and after the Great Recession due to the artificial ascendance of a growth-driven agenda and finance-sector regulation around the world. The fourth is whether financialization matters only for developed economies (Bonizzi, 2013; Bortz & Kaltenbrunner, 2018; Demir, 2009). A key limitation in investigating these four trends is that a clear-cut definition of financialization is still lacking in such a way that its system-wide impact is clarified, not only for developed economies but also, and in particular, for developing economies.

Given these four themes, this book makes six contributions and analytic implications. In line with the heterodox approach, it first aims to define financialization in terms of (i) its bilateral interaction with the major components of real economy and (ii) its direct and indirect impact on labor's share of aggregate income or the compensation of labor by dominating real economic activity. Second, the book investigates the finance-growth nexus by disaggregating the major components of real economic activity into government purchases, investment expenditures, private consumption expenditures, exports, imports, foreign direct inflows, and foreign direct outflows. In doing so, the book investigates financialization at the level of the real economic system by

DOI: 10.4324/9781003336105-1

bringing all these components of real economy into the analysis simultaneously in terms of their individual and joint relationships with aggregate financial development, financial organizational development, and financial market development.

Third, as a corollary, the book uses the recently introduced and the most comprehensive proxy of financial development that covers the three major components of financial development – depth, efficiency, and access – into an analysis of aggregate financial development, financial organizational development, and financial market development. Fourth, the book uses the Panel Vector Auto Regressive Model (Panel VAR) and Panel Granger Causality test to investigate the real economy-finance-labor nexus for high-income countries (HICs), and the real economy-finance nexus for upper-middle-income (UMICs) and lower-middle-income countries (LMICs). Fifth, the book examines both the real economy-finance-labor nexus and the real economy-finance nexus not only for the entire period 1980–2018 but also for the periods before and after the Great Recession, 1980–2007 and 2008–2018. This comparative analysis will illustrate the potential effects of the Great Recession of 2008–2009 and the Great or Secular Stagnation of 2010–2018 on the real economy-finance-labor nexus. Sixth, the book introduces a disaggregated analysis of financialization by breaking it down into three types: *fundamental*, *regressive*, and *structural*.

Chapter 1 of the book attempts to explain financialization's economics to both economists and non-economists. The process of financialization has been studied primarily by non-economists, while the texts written by economists on the topic emphasize sophisticated technical details. There appears to be a need for a systemic explanation of the economics of financialization for non-economists to comprehend the relationships between the economy and finance. This context is also necessary for economists, as economics textbooks do not explain the economy-finance nexus in the systemic way that this book does. The first proceeds to explain the real economy-finance, real economy-labor, and finance-labor nexus at the level of economic systems in order to illustrate that financialization is a systemic dynamic that influences the two basic pillars of an economic regime, real economic output, and its distribution among the factors of production. Chapter 2 defines financialization with a structured literature review, lays out the potential for change in the nexus before and after the Great Recession, and introduces the analytic frame to be used for empirical estimation. Chapter 3 introduces the empirical methodology and data, and discusses empirical findings for three groups of countries (high-income, upper-middle-income, and lower-middle-income countries) first using yearly data for the periods 1980–2018, 1980–2007, and 2008–2018 and second zooming in the periods of Great Recession (2008Q1–2009Q4) and Secular Stagnation (2010Q1–2021Q3) using quarterly data.

References

Arcand, J. L., Berkes, E., and Panizza, U. 2015. Too much finance? *Journal of Economic Growth*, *20*(2), 105–148.

Bonizzi, B. 2013. Financialization in developing and emerging countries: A survey. *International Journal of Political Economy*, *42*(4), 83–107.

Bortz, P. G., and Kaltenbrunner, A. 2018. The international dimension of financialization in developing and emerging economies. *Development and Change*, *49*(2), 375–393.

Demir, F. 2009. Financial liberalization, private investment and portfolio choice: Financialization of real sectors in emerging markets. *Journal of Development Economics*, *88*(2), 314–324.

Krippner, G. R. 2005. The financialization of the American economy. *Socio-Economic Review*, *3*(2), 173–208.

Law, S. H., and Singh, N. 2014. Does too much finance harm economic growth? *Journal of Banking and Finance*, *41*, 36–44.

Shen, C.-H., and Lee, C.-C. 2006. Same financial development yet different economic growth: Why? *Journal of Money, Credit and Banking*, *38*(7), 1907–1944.

Van der Zwan, N. 2014. Making sense of financialization. *Socio-Economic Review*, *12*(1), 99–129.

1 The Economics of Financialization for Economists and Noneconomists

This section clarifies four topics. First is the primary component of an economic system. Second is their interaction with one another. Third is how economic models can be classified for a comprehensive analysis. Fourth is how they can be restructured to understand financialization as an issue affecting the entire economy.

The section will proceed in a step-by-step format that is primarily accessible to non-economists. It is necessary for two purposes. First, the literature on financialization is dominated by qualitatively oriented political economists, political scientists, and sociologists, as financialization is not only an economic phenomenon but also a political and sociological phenomenon, necessitating a qualitative approach. Therefore, a multi-disciplinary approach is required for an in-depth comprehension, which can typically be attained through a qualitative approach. Second, financialization is an economic issue at its core, and its quantitative dynamics must be captured for a complete understanding. Consequently, due to the multidisciplinary character of financialization, qualitative and quantitative explanations are not mutually exclusive but rather complementary. Beginning with a qualitative description of the economic system's behavior that is accessible to both economists and non-economists, this section is essential for comprehending the financialization process.

This qualitative context will be used in the following sections to develop quantitative models for estimating the dynamics of financialization across economic systems. After qualitatively understanding macroeconomy-finance relationships, non-economist students of financialization can comprehend the structure of quantitative methods and their outcomes with relative ease.

1.1 Understanding Economic and Financial Systems

1.1.1 What Is an Economic System?

The term "economic system" refers, in broad terms, to all elements of an economy that support its operation. The combination of these elements to attain a specific objective is what makes an economy a system. As shown in Figure 1.1,

DOI: 10.4324/9781003336105-2

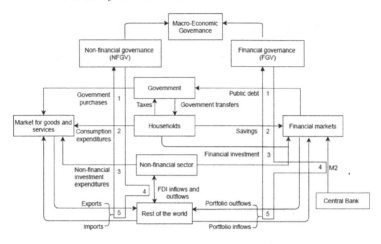

Figure 1.1 Macro-Financial and Nonfinancial Governance.

Source: Akan et al. (2021).

an economic system consists primarily of financial and nonfinancial components. The objective of financial components is to provide the necessary financial inputs for nonfinancial activities. Nonfinancial elements are geared toward achieving economic production and consumption. For example, households transfer their savings to the financial system in the form of deposits, the financial system uses these deposits to issue loans to their individual or institutional customers, and the customers use these loans for consumption or investment purposes. This economic cycle is a straightforward example of how financial and nonfinancial elements of an economic system interact.

The categorization of economic activities as "financial" and "non-financial" facilitates an orderly comprehension of an economic system through these two divisions. This is necessary because financialization is a complex issue involving both nonfinancial and financial aspects of an economic system. Without a structured understanding of these components, a student of financialization may become disoriented by the complexities and unpredictability of their interrelationships. The initial step in forming this impression could be to consider that "financial" and "nonfinancial" dynamics could be either macro or micro.

Examples of macro-financial and macro-nonfinancial components of an economic system include aggregate savings and aggregate economic growth because their scope incorporates systemic economic dynamics rather than individual ones. All economic units, including governments, businesses (corporate and non-corporate), and households, accumulate aggregate savings, or economic growth is attained by all these three entities and the rest of the world. Similarly, micro-financial and nonfinancial components include financial markets and nonfinancial firms' investment expenditures because financial markets are one of many market structures, such as commodity and labor markets. Investment expenditures by nonfinancial enterprises are one of the four components of economic growth, along with government purchases, household consumption expenditures, and net exports.

Understanding how an economic system is governed is the second stage in forming an organized impression of an economic system as economic governance is an essential mechanism for integrating financial and nonfinancial components. Economic governance can be defined, in broad strokes, as a patterned or unpatterned system of institution-mediated interaction between public or private actors for adjusting or monitoring one or more market structures under the guidance of predetermined rules and procedures (Akan et al., 2023). In terms of the overall conduct of a macroeconomic system, economic governance can be financial and nonfinancial. Financial and nonfinancial governance aims to govern financial and nonfinancial components in an economic system. Financialization is a process at the crossroads of these two types of governance.

Macro-financial and macro-nonfinancial governance are defined in Table 1.1. Their components are also explained in Table 1.1. A key determinant of a country's overall economic performance is how these aggregates are governed or organized. In terms of the governance of economic structures, we posit three modes of economic governance: systemic governance, fragmentation, and structural traps. The variety of these modes depends on the complementary or discomplementary linkages between their underlying dynamics. Furthermore, the mode of governance shifts economic performance by establishing or disrupting (macro-micro) complementarities between economic actors and markets. Specifically, we suggest that a systemic mode of governance improves economic performance, the introduction or deepening of fragmentation and the consequent structural trap arising out of disrupting or eliminating complementarities will worsen economic performance.

Complementarities can be defined as the mutual reinforcement among a certain group of aggregates in part or all of a social structure that improves or worsens clustering relative to alternative configurations (Akan et al., 2023; Hall & Soskice, 2001). For example, the postwar West German model was drawn upon, *inter alia*, a fiscal and monetary policy targeting full employment; a stakeholder system in managing industrial investment, technological progress, workforce training, and international competitiveness; optimally high aggregate savings, long-term and targeted investment finance based on joint stock-sharing, and high fixed-capital investment; and efficiency wages defined as high labor productivity and high real wages. These complementarities enabled the country to establish and sustain the synergy of productive solidarity among high economic growth, rapid industrial sophistication, and

Table 1.1 The Components of Macroeconomic Governance.

Macroeconomic governance, $MEG = f(NFGV, FGV)$

Macro-nonfinancial governance, $NFGV = f(GEXD, PINV, PCNS, TRD, FDI)$

Macro-nonfinancial governance	Abbreviations	Macro-nonfinancial governance is a policy mix consisting of the propensity of
Government expenditures	*GEXD*	governments to adjust the size of their purchases
Private investment expenditures	*PINV*	nonfinancial investors to adjust the size of fixed-capital investment
Private consumption exp.	*PCNS*	households and non-profit organizations to adjust the size of personal consumption
International trade	*TRD*	nonfinancial businesses to adjust the size of imports or exports
Foreign direct investment	*FDI*	foreign direct investors to adjust the size of their investments across countries.

Macro-financial governance, $FGV = f(PBDT, M2, SVG, PINV, FVA)$

Macro-financial governance	Abbreviations	Macro-financial governance is a policy mix consisting of the propensity of
Public debt	*PBDT*	governments to adjust the size of debt securities for financing their purchases
Money	*M2*	central banks to adopt an accommodative or non-accommodative monetary policy mainly by changing the *quantity* of money
Savings	*SVG*	households to use their savings to buy financial assets such as debt securities, corporate equities, and mutual fund shares, or depositing their money as time and savings deposits
Portfolio investment	*PRTF*	local or foreign portfolio investors to transfer their funds across countries
Financial value-added	*FVA*	value added by the finance sector in proportion to the manufacturing sector

Source: Adapted from Akan et al. (2023).

relatively low-income inequality, particularly from the early 1950s till the early 1990s (Streeck, 1997).

1.1.2 What Is a Financial System?

Understanding financialization requires positing a financial system into an economic system. Figure 1.1 already depicts a financial system in an economic system. However, there is a need for further explanation for comprehending how it interacts with the other elements of that system.

System of National Accounts (SNA) is a framework covering all major aspects of economic and financial development (van de Ven & Fano, 2017). The Organization for Economic Cooperation and Development (OECD), the

European Union, the International Monetary Fund (IMF), and the Federal Reserve System (FED) have all adopted SNA. The framework is based on the idea that an economic system comprises numerous macroeconomic and financial transactions executed by institutional units engaged in economic activities, such as production, consumption, and trading, as well as the accumulation, exchange, and management of financial assets and liabilities. These institutional units with similar functions are grouped by the SNA into five main institutional sectors: financial corporations, nonfinancial corporations, general government, households and non-profit institutions serving households, and the rest of the world.

These sectors lend or borrow available funds from financial markets or financial institutions in order to finance the production and consumption activities that are the foundation of economic growth. Financial system consists of two elements: financial corporations and financial markets. Financial corporations consist of monetary financial corporations and other financial corporations. Monetary financial corporations are central banks, deposit-taking corporations, and money market funds (MMF). Other financial corporations are non-MMF investment funds, insurance corporations, and pension funds. Financial markets consist of stock markets, bond markets, money markets, foreign exchange markets, and derivative markets.

Lending sectors (nonfinancial corporations, the general government, households, and the rest of the world) deposit money in deposit-taking institutions, issue debt instruments, demand money, borrow loans, receive credits, guarantee their financial or nonfinancial assets, etc. Central banks influence output growth by issuing and controlling the quantity, flow, and cost of money through money supply and reserve requirements, by purchasing governmental or private debt securities on primary or secondary markets, and by assisting commercial banks with emergency liquidity to meet money demand for transaction purposes, among other methods.

Deposit-taking banks extend loans to nonfinancial players and mostly invest in long-term debt securities. MMF raise capital through the issuance of shares as a source of investment in short-term liquid assets, repurchase agreements, or short-term debt securities, and the repayment of shares upon demand. Non-MMF funds raise capital through the issuance of shares and invest in longer-term investments such as stocks, bonds, and real estate. For employees and the self-employed, insurance companies and pension funds provide insurance (non-life insurance, life insurance and annuities, reinsurance, social insurance schemes, and standardized guarantee schemes) and pension systems, respectively. Providing income upon retirement and financial relief in the event of death, disability, injury, etc., both institutions are key collectors of savings and providers of cash to financial markets by investing mostly in debt instruments and shares. In terms of the growth-finance nexus, both nonfinancial firms and governments issue bonds in financial markets to fund business investment and government deficits, respectively, whereas only nonfinancial corporations issue stocks. Real economic actors and financial companies such as banks purchase and sell these stocks and bonds to fund their loan assets (van de Ven & Fano, 2017).

1.1.2.1 How Do the Economic and Financial Systems Interact?

This section aims to explain how financial and economic systems interact. We focus on nonfinancial economic structures and financial systems and take these structures as "real economy" for simplicity. The reason why we focus on real economy is the fact that there are three major issues in the debate on contemporary economies in terms of the real economy-finance nexus. First, the real economy has become financialized. Second, financialized real economic activity suppresses labor. Third, the finance sector suppresses labor. The explanation of this nexus, real economy-finance-equality of income in the context of these debates requires investigating (i) the effect of financial system on real economic activity, (ii) the effect of real economic activity on the equality of income, and (ii) the relationship between real economy and financial system.

To make this investigation, we reorganize Figure 1.1 in Figure 1.2 to demonstrate the relationships between finance, real economy, and the inequality of income. We take compensation of employees (COEs) as a proxy for inequality of income. There are three prerequisites of this explanation.

The first is to bring real economic activity into an analysis of the *structure of growth* rather than only of aggregate growth itself or a few of its constituent variables. As illustrated in Figure 1.2, the totality of real economic activity comprises public and private consumption, public and private investment, imports, exports, foreign direct inflows, and foreign direct outflows. Measuring real economic activity by summing the quantities of government purchases, private investment, private consumption, and net exports (exports

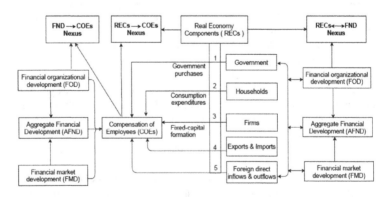

Figure 1.2 RECs-FND-COEs Nexus.

minus imports) as advised by technical macroeconomics bypasses the overall impact of imports and exports. Neither does it include foreign direct outflows. A change in the quantity of foreign direct outflows has the potential to significantly impact a country's economic governance; it can increase or decrease total domestic output and employment, the size of domestic financial markets, available funds for nonfinancial investment, and asset prices or interest rates. In the same vein, when we only take net exports into account, we calculate the income impact of import and export activities, either positively or negatively. However, when we take the total quantities of both imports and exports, we assess the entire impact of both on investment, consumption, output, and on the size of financial markets or the total assets of financial organizations in terms of the quantity of debt securities or equities issued by importers or exporters, or the quantity of investment credits demanded by them.

The second is to bring into the analysis the components of real economy and aggregate financial development, the components of real economy and financial institutional development, and the components of real economy and financial market development separately, which is necessary to cover the overall and disaggregated effects of the finance sector both on real economy and the inequality of income. As featured by the Great Recession, (i) the operations of all financial corporations and all financial assets on their balance sheets, ranging from equity and loans to MMF shares and financial derivatives, (ii) the total size and composition of stock and securities markets, and, first and foremost, (iii) how effective all financial and nonfinancial corporations use the financial assets on their balance sheets matter for economic growth and the equality of income (Beck, 2012; van de Ven & Fano, 2017). The financial development index (Svirydzenka, 2016) allows bringing these three dynamics of finance into the analysis altogether. The index is an aggregate of the financial organizational index and the financial markets index, the implications of which are illustrated in Table 1.2. Evidently, both indices also allow us to disaggregate the impact of aggregate financial development on real economy and the inequality of income.

The third prerequisite is the COEs, which *"consists of all payments in cash, as well as in kind (such as food and housing), to employees in return for services rendered, and government contributions to social insurance schemes such as social security and pensions that provide benefits to employees"* (World Bank, 2021). Employee compensation is paid by firms to workers or is the factor of labor out of aggregate income that firms receive through their sales in the market for goods and services; that is, it is the pretax labor income share of aggregate income or GDP. Thus, it is the most comprehensive proxy for investigating the growth-finance-labor nexus as it indicates the functional distribution of income between capital and labor at the level of the economic system. Another key reason to use the COEs is its availability for a sufficient number of countries in a statistically consistent manner for cross-country research for the period 1980–2018.[1]

Table 1.2 The Coverage of Financial Organizations Index and Financial Markets Index.

	1. Financial organizations index
1.a. Financial organizational depth index	Bank credit to the private sector in percent of GDP, pension fund assets to GDP, mutual fund assets to GDP, and insurance premiums, life and non-life to GDP.
1.b. Financial organization efficiency index	Banking sector net interest margin, lending-deposit spread, non-interest income to total income, overhead costs to total assets, return on assets, and return on equity.
1.c. Financial institutions access index	Bank branches per 100,000 adults and ATMs per 100,000 adults.
	2. Financial markets index
2.a. Financial markets depth index	Stock market capitalization to GDP, international debt securities of government to GDP, and total debt securities of financial and nonfinancial corporations to GDP
2.b. Financial markets efficiency index	Stock market turnover ratio (stocks traded to capitalization)
2.c. Financial markets access index	Percent of market capitalization outside of the top 10 largest companies and total number of issuers of debt (domestic and external, nonfinancial and financial corporations) per 100,000 adults.

Source: Svirydzenka (2016).

In the remaining of this chapter, we provide an intense and systematic review of all three nexuses in order to illustrate the complex relationships between financialization, real output, and the inequality of income.

1.1.3   Real Economy-Finance Nexus

Real economic actors (governments, private businesses, consumers, and foreign direct investors) may stimulate or de-stimulate financial development by demanding a higher or lower quantity of loans, by issuing a higher or lower number of corporate bonds, stocks or government bonds, or by using a higher or lower portion of their disposable income for investment in financial assets. In the case of de-stimulation, all four economic actors may finance nonfinancial activity using their savings, firms using more equity capital or excess profits, governments imposing higher taxes, workers using higher wage earnings, etc. Cheaper imports due to, for example, currency depreciation in the foreign countries or appreciation in the importing country or to the lifting or lowering of tariffs or quotas may require obtaining less debt for enterprises and households. Outward foreign direct investors may stimulate financial development by using domestic financial resources for their investment abroad or de-stimulate it by transferring their financial assets or investment to a foreign financial market, respectively.

In addition to the components of real economy, we will use two control variables in investigating the nexus between real economy, financial development, and the inequality of income because inflation may de-stimulate financial development by eroding the real value of financial wealth and assets or stimulate it by requiring households and governments to use more loans because of their declining purchasing power. Total factor productivity may stimulate financial development by increasing the demand for corporate stocks due to increased profitability, causing higher unemployment and demand for bank credits by workers or de-stimulate it by reducing the need for loans by firms due to increased profitability and lower costs of production or by working consumers, thanks to rising real wages in parallel with rising labor productivity.

Financial development can stimulate real economic activity by (i) issuing more low-cost and long-term credits or funding higher quantities of government and corporate bonds, paving the way for greater production and consumption; (ii) accumulating capital and improving resource allocation by transferring funds to more productive, viable, and profitable investments; and (iii) facilitating trading, hedging, diversifying, and pooling risk, thereby stimulating higher levels of capital formation and efficiency particularly for small companies, higher quantities of investment and consumption, greater international competitiveness, and faster and more sophisticated technological innovation. Financial development can stimulate total factor productivity by providing firms with cheaper, faster, and long-term financial funds, inspiring productivity-oriented investments (Ductor & Grechyna, 2015; Greenwood & Jovanovic, 1990; Hall & Soskice, 2001; Han & Shen, 2015; Levine, 2002; Streeck, 1997; Tori & Onaran, 2020).

Financial development may de-stimulate real economic activity by (i) requiring economic actors to make high-interest payments or get debt to roll over their accumulated debts, leaving less room for investment and consumption; (ii) generating less income for real economic actors from investments in financial assets or from stocks, particularly during times of financial instability and economic crisis, underlying lower aggregate demand; and (iii) inciting a shareholder mode of corporate governance and short-term financial performance and returns on capital investment rather than on long-run productivity, facilitating takeovers for short-term financial gains, picking up unviable enterprises and consumers, extending and socializing the risk of asset-price bubbles and financial sunk costs due to irrational exuberance, all of which result in resource misallocation and lower efficiency, massive wealth destruction and an aggregate demand gap (Al-Yousif, 2002; Calderón & Liu, 2003; Demetriades & Hussein, 1996; Orhangazi, 2008; Rajan, 2006; Tomaskovic-Devey et al., 2015; Tori & Onaran, 2020).

There would also be no relationships between real economy and financial development. The main reasons for this include (i) a low or excessively high level of financial depth; (ii) financial crises, particularly when there were bank credit booms prior to the crisis; (iii) that economies catch up to the global technological frontier; (iv) poor institutions; (v) double-digit inflation; and (vi) the short-run nature of relationships (Aghion et al., 2005; Aisen & Franken, 2010; Christopoulos & Tsionas, 2004; De Gregorio & Guidotti, 1995; Deidda & Fattouh, 2008; Demetriades & Hussein, 1996; Rioja & Valev, 2004; Rousseau & Wachtel, 2011).

1.1.4   The Real Economy-Labor Nexus

Higher aggregate income due to an increase in aggregate demand or output (consumption, investment, exports, inward foreign direct investment) may stimulate the COEs on condition of efficiency wages. Government purchases (investment and consumption expenditures) can stimulate or de-stimulate COEs directly by increasing and decreasing payments to social insurance schemes or indirectly by creating a positive and negative multiplier impact on aggregate output and income, respectively. Private investment expenditures can stimulate COEs by creating more jobs and increasing real wages, thanks to rising profitability or declining costs (economies of scale), and de-stimulate them by substituting labor with capital and reducing workers' real wages (Basu & Guariglia, 2007; Stack, 1978).

Higher quantities of exports and imports may be a source of higher or lower employment and income for workers, depending on the existence or lack of efficiency wages, the prices of exports and imports, and the real effective exchange rate. More and less income by high- and low-value-added exports, or by low- and high-cost imports in the case of low and high real effective exchange rates, stimulate higher and lower income for firms, respectively, as a potential source of increased or decreased compensation for employees, respectively (Alderson & Nielsen, 2002; Dreher & Gaston, 2008; Harrison, 2002; Lee et al., 2007). Inflation can stimulate and de-stimulate COEs by providing higher income to firms and by increasing production costs due to the rising prices of intermediate goods, respectively. Total factor productivity stimulates the COEs by a potential increase in wages because of higher labor productivity and rising aggregate income of firms, or de-stimulates it by enabling the production of the same quantity of goods and services using a lower labor factor, reducing the share of labor income, respectively.

1.1.5   Finance-Labor Nexus

Financial development can stimulate and de-stimulate COEs by its positive and negative effects on real economic activity due to factoring into higher and lower aggregate demand and supply as a potential source of more and less income for the factor of labor, respectively. The rise in financial value-added increases the wealth and income of financial workers and affluent households, aggravating income disparity, by increasing returns to the factor of capital and executive compensation as well as by excluding the production work-force from revenue-generating and compensation-setting processes (Edmans et al., 2012; Godechot, 2012; Lee, 2006; Lin & Tomaskovic-Devey, 2013; Tomaskovic-Devey & Lin, 2011).

The sector can also affect COEs through financialized real economic structures. If private businesses or households use a significant portion of their incomes to make financial investments instead of to produce and consume, or governments use a significant portion of taxes to pay off the capital and interest of their debts as a stimulus for financialization, COEs will be lower due to declining aggregate demand and to the resulting higher unemployment and lower wage income in parallel with the declining profitability of manufacturing enterprises. In addition, the nonfinancial firms that adopt a shareholder mode of governance deunionize and lay off production workers massively and substitute the factor of labor with capital factor (Assa, 2012; Fligstein & Goldstein, 2015; Godechot, 2016; Kus, 2012; Kuttner, 2008; Palley, 2013; Roberts & Kwon, 2017; Zalewski & Whalen, 2010).

It is argued that financial development can alleviate inequality of income by increasing credit access for less affluent households, allowing them to invest in education or new business opportunities (Clarke et al., 2006; Greenwood & Jovanovic, 1990; Nikoloski, 2013; Roberts & Kwon, 2017). However, financial access is only part of financial development. The steady access of less affluent households to funds is apparently subject to an equal distribution of income, as easier or faster access to credit might place their financial sustainability at risk without a parallel increase in their real income, an underlying reason for the Great Recession.

Note

1 Gini index may be considered as a more comprehensive proxy as it measures the equality of the distribution of income between all households of various income groups. However, first, we concentrate on the impact of finance and financialized economic structures on labor, and second, the Gini coefficient data are either not available for a sufficiently long period of time for a robust econometric modeling or are available for a limited number of countries.

References

Aghion, P., Angeletos, G.-M., Banerjee, A., and Manova, K. 2005. *Volatility and growth: Credit constraints and productivity-enhancing investment.* National Bureau of Economic Research Cambridge, MA, USA.

Aisen, M. A., and Franken, M. 2010. *Bank credit during the 2008 financial crisis: A cross-country comparison.* International Monetary Fund, Washington, DC.

Akan, T., Hepsag, A., Bozoklu, S., and Mollaahmetoğlu, E. 2023. Finance as a friend, enemy and stranger in the US economy, 1952–2019. *Socio-Economic Review, 21*(1), 397–435.

Alderson, A. S., and Nielsen, F. 2002. Globalization and the great U-turn: Income inequality trends in 16 OECD countries. *American Journal of Sociology, 107*(5), 1244–1299.

Al-Yousif, Y. K. 2002. Financial development and economic growth: Another look at the evidence from developing countries. *Review of Financial Economics, 11*(2), 131–150.

Assa, J. 2012. Financialization and its consequences: The OECD experience. *Finance Research, 1*(1), 35–39.

Basu, P., and Guariglia, A. 2007. Foreign direct investment, inequality, and growth. *Journal of Macroeconomics, 29*(4), 824–839.

Beck, T. 2012. Finance and growth–lessons from the literature and the recent crisis. *LSE Growth Commission, 3*, 1–6.

Calderón, C., and Liu, L. 2003. The direction of causality between financial development and economic growth. *Journal of Development Economics, 72*(1), 321–334.

Christopoulos, D. K., and Tsionas, E. G. 2004. Financial development and economic growth: Evidence from panel unit root and cointegration tests. *Journal of Development Economics, 73*(1), 55–74.

Clarke, G. R., Xu, L. C., and Zou, H.-F. 2006. Finance and income inequality: What do the data tell us? *Southern Economic Journal, 72*(3), 578–596.

De Gregorio, J., and Guidotti, P. E. 1995. Financial development and economic growth. *World Development, 23*(3), 433–448.

Deidda, L., and Fattouh, B. 2008. Banks, financial markets and growth. *Journal of Financial Intermediation, 17*(1), 6–36.

Demetriades, P. O., and Hussein, K. A. 1996. Does financial development cause economic growth? Time-series evidence from 16 countries. *Journal of Development Economics, 51*(2), 387–411.

Dreher, A., and Gaston, N. 2008. Has globalization increased inequality? *Review of International Economics, 16*(3), 516–536.

Ductor, L., and Grechyna, D. 2015. Financial development, real sector, and economic growth. *International Review of Economics and Finance, 37*, 393–405.

Edmans, A., Goldstein, I., and Jiang, W. 2012. The real effects of financial markets: The impact of prices on takeovers. *The Journal of Finance, 67*(3), 933–971.

Fligstein, N., and Goldstein, A. 2015. The emergence of a finance culture in American households, 1989–2007. *Socio-Economic Review, 13*(3), 575–601.

Godechot, O. 2012. Is finance responsible for the rise in wage inequality in France? *Socio-Economic Review, 10*(3), 447–470.

Godechot, O. 2016. Financialization is marketization! A study of the respective impacts of various dimensions of financialization on the increase in global inequality. *Sociological Science, 3*, 495–519.

Greenwood, J., and Jovanovic, B. 1990. Financial development, growth, and the distribution of income. *Journal of Political Economy, 98*(5), 1076–1107.

Hall, P. A., and Soskice, D. 2001. *The institutional foundations of comparative advantage.* Oxford University Press, New York, NY.

Han, J., and Shen, Y. 2015. Financial development and total factor productivity growth: Evidence from China. *Emerging Markets Finance and Trade, 51*, 261–274.

Harrison, A. 2002. *Has globalization eroded labor's share. Some cross-country evidence.* UC Berkeley and NBER.

Kus, B. 2012. Financialisation and income inequality in OECD nations: 1995–2007. *The Economic and Social Review, 43*(4), 477–495.

Kuttner, R. 2008. *The squandering of America: How the failure of our politics undermines our prosperity*. Vintage: New York.

Lee, J.-E. 2006. Inequality and globalization in Europe. *Journal of Policy Modeling*, *28*(7), 791–796.

Lee, C.-S., Nielsen, F., and Alderson, A. S. 2007. Income inequality, global economy and the state. *Social Forces*, *86*(1), 77–111.

Levine, R. 2002. Bank-based or market-based financial systems: Which is better? *Journal of Financial Intermediation*, *11*(4), 398–428.

Lin, K.-H., and Tomaskovic-Devey, D. 2013. Financialization and US income inequality, 1970–2008. *American Journal of Sociology*, *118*(5), 1284–1329.

Nikoloski, Z. 2013. Financial sector development and inequality: Is there a financial Kuznets curve? *Journal of International Development*, *25*(7), 897–911.

OECD. 2014. *Does income inequality hurt economic growth? Focus on inequality and growth*. OECD Publishing, Paris.

Orhangazi, Ö. 2008. Financialisation and capital accumulation in the non-financial corporate sector: A theoretical and empirical investigation on the US economy: 1973–2003. *Cambridge Journal of Economics*, *32*(6), 863–886.

Palley, T. I. 2013. Financialization: What it is and why it matters. In *Financialization* (pp. 17–40). New York: Springer.

Rajan, R. G. 2006. Has finance made the world riskier? *European Financial Management*, *12*(4), 499–533.

Rioja, F., and Valev, N. 2004. Finance and the sources of growth at various stages of economic development. *Economic Inquiry*, *42*(1), 127–140.

Roberts, A., and Kwon, R. 2017. Finance, inequality and the varieties of capitalism in post-industrial democracies. *Socio-Economic Review*, *15*(3), 511–538.

Rousseau, P. L., and Wachtel, P. 2011. What is happening to the impact of financial deepening on economic growth? *Economic Inquiry*, *49*(1), 276–288.

Stack, S. 1978. The effect of direct government involvement in the economy on the degree of income inequality: A cross-national study. *American Sociological Review*, *43*(6), 880–888.

Streeck, W. 1997. German Capitalism: Does it exist? Can it survive? *New Political Economy*, *2*(2), 237–256.

Svirydzenka, K. 2016. *Introducing a new broad-based index of financial development*. Washington, DC: International Monetary Fund.

Tomaskovic-Devey, D., and Lin, K.-H. 2011. Income dynamics, economic rents, and the financialization of the US economy. *American Sociological Review*, *76*(4), 538–559.

Tomaskovic-Devey, D., Lin, K.-H., and Meyers, N. 2015. Did financialization reduce economic growth? *Socio-Economic Review*, *13*(3), 525–548.

Tori, D., and Onaran, Ö. 2020. Financialization, financial development and investment. Evidence from European non-financial corporations. *Socio-Economic Review*, *18*(3), 681–718.

van de Ven, P., and Fano, D. (2017). *Understanding financial accounts*. OECD Publishing, Paris.

World Bank. 2021. *World development indicators*. Available from: https://databank.worldbank.org/source/world-development-indicators [10 May 2020].

Zalewski, D. A., and Whalen, C. J. 2010. Financialization and income inequality: A post Keynesian institutionalist analysis. *Journal of Economic Issues*, *44*(3), 757–777.

2 Defining Financialization and Its Varieties

2.1 Financialization: Fundamental, Regressive, and Structural

Given the trilateral and complex relationships encompassing the real economy-finance-labor nexus, we define financialization as a process in which (i) real economic activity stimulates financial development (FND), (ii) but FND either does not stimulate or negatively stimulates real economic activity, and (iii) FND and financialized real economic structure separately or jointly suppress labor or aggravate the inequality of income over a certain period. This definition rests upon a simple fact: the finance sector exists to serve real economic activity and financialization emerges when the finance sector turns into a "growth sector in itself" (Beck, 2012), in which case, the finance sector is highly likely to impede growth.

The first two conditions are enough to identify financialization as they illustrate the transformation of the finance sector into a growth sector in itself. The third condition also holds because the negative impact of the finance sector on the real economy and inequality of income are complementary. We can define a process of financialization that lies in the first two conditions and in all three conditions as *fundamental* and *structural*, respectively. *Structural financialization* refers to the fact that the finance sector de-stimulates real economy and the compensation of labor as the main indicators of economic efficiency and equality, respectively, which are the two basic pillars upon which economic structure rests.

The third kind of financialization is *regressive* financialization that emerges when the finance sector itself of a financialized real economic structure suppresses labor, which rests upon these facts. First, the finance sector may distribute an increasing share of financial gains to capital owners rather than to labor, *direcly* regressing the compensation of employees. Second, a financialized real economic structure may distribute an increasing share of total income to capital owners rather than to labor. In the second case, the finance sector *indirectly* regresses the compensation of employees through financialized economic structure.

DOI: 10.4324/9781003336105-3

In the existing literature, there are three entrenched definitions of financialization: (i) as a regime of accumulation to extract profits at the macro level, a new model of corporate governance at the meso level, and the major motive of investing subjects as the economic citizens in a risk society (Van der Zwan, 2014); (ii) "*the increasing role of financial motives, financial markets, financial actors and financial institutions in the operation of the domestic and international economies*" (Esptein, 2005: 3); and (iii) a pattern of accumulation in which profits accrue primarily through financial channels rather than through trade and commodities (Krippner, 2005). This book emphasizes the need for a clear-cut definition that can be measured using a systematic qualitative and quantitative set of data. Our definition might be regarded as a preliminary attempt to make such a definition, which is limited to economic systems using a similar approach to Epstein's, but, unlike Zwan's, does not cover political or social dynamics.

An analysis of financialization based on our definition is applicable to developing economies, too. We apply our analysis for three groups of countries: high-income, upper-middle-income, and lower-middle-income countries (HICs, UMICs, and LMICs, respectively). The income-based approach is relevant regarding the outright differences between all three kinds of FND levels in HICs, UMICs, and LMICs, as illustrated in Table 2.1. However, our approach does not take it for granted that there is or is not a variety of capitalism[1] but aims to illustrate (i) that the level of FND or the modes of macroeconomic governance may underlie both similar or diverse modes of real economy-finance-labor nexus, (ii) there might be both positive complementarities (PCMTs) or negative complementarities (NCMTs), for example, in stimulating or de-stimulating FND and the inequality of income (We avoid any a priori theoretical bias), and (iii) beyond rationalist-functionalism (Streeck, 2018), the nexus may have incurred changes in all three country groups particularly after the Great Recession when neo-classical regimes of macroeconomic governance had evolved into a policy trap, which is elaborated on below.

Our definition is apparently at odds with the hypothesis of a U-shaped growth-finance nexus, in that it rests upon explaining financialization in terms of its fundamental, regressive, and structural functions, to serve the real economy and not to harm workers' or the wealth of less-affluent households.

Table 2.1 The Level of Financial Development*.

	AFND	*FOD*	*FMD*
HICs	0.61	0.68	0.52
UMICs	0.33	0.44	0.21
LMICs	0.22	0.28	0.15

*Index value ranges between 0 and 1 (IMF, 2021).

Specifying a threshold below or above which the finance sector starts benefiting or harming real economic activity might not be an end in itself. For example, we find evidence for financialization in LMICs but not in UMICs. Neither can such a conclusion be explained by the threshold effect or the U-shaped finance-growth hypothesis. Nor can specific policy proposals be suggested for LMICs to harness the finance sector based on the findings of the U-shaped hypothesis. Any proposal such as "LMICs should restrain finance sector growth" or "LMICs should further promote finance sector growth" will not be relevant. Because FND is already in its infancy in these countries and growth is necessary for a stable and sustainable increase in aggregate income, financialization well illustrates that its growth in LMICs is highly unlikely to promote real economic activity.

Instead, it should first be established which components of real economy underlie financialization, why, and how. Second, the components underlying financialization can be reorganized in such a way so as to restrain further financialization without unnecessarily disrupting the orderly growth of the aggregate finance sector. The third step, as a corollary, is to disaggregate financialization by examining the relationships between real economy and each of aggregate financial development (AFND), financial organizational development (FOD), and financial market development (FMD). The disaggregation of AFND is necessary to pinpoint the growth-inhibiting, growth-enhancing, or inequality-increasing aspects of the finance sector, which would be significant at the stage of policy formulation and development.

2.2 Great Recession, Secular Stagnation, and Financialization

As Table 2.2 illustrates, in comparison to 1980–2007, in the 2008–2018 period, GDP growth plummeted, the pace of growth in AFND, FOD, and FMD turned negative, but the rate of growth in the compensation of employees turned positive, albeit slightly, in HICs. In UMICs, too, the pace of growth of GDP, AFND, FOD, and FMD slowed down remarkably during and after the Great Recession. LMICs diverge from HICs and UMICs as the rate of growth of all these four indicators, in particular of FMD, increased considerably in the period 2008–2018. Evidently, the rates of negative or positive changes in FOD and FMD for all country groups diverge from each other. Thus, the quantitative evolution of the components of real economy, each type of FND (AFND, FMD, and FOD), and compensation of employees point to a need for making a comparative analysis of the real economy-finance-labor nexus, including a separate analysis of the growth of AFND, FOD, and FMD between the periods 1980–2007 and 2008–2018. It might be beyond the scope of this book to elaborate on the dynamics of change in all these five variables in each country group, as it is a matter of empirical analysis. However, what is worth noting is that the need for a comparison of the change in the five variables

Table 2.2 Annual Changes in GDP, FND, and COEs.

	GDP	AFND	FOD	FMD	COEs
			HICs		
1980–2018	2.5	2.4	1.3	4.3	−0.1
1980–2007	3.0	3.5	2.0	6.2	−0.2
2008–2018	1.2	−0.4	−0.5	−0.3	0.2
			UMICs		
1980–2018	3.8	1.7	1.5	3.1	...
1980–2007	4.1	1.8	1.6	3.5	...
2008–2018	3.1	1.3	1.3	2.2	...
			LMICs		
1980–2018	4.2	1.6	1.7	3.1	...
1980–2007	4.0	1.5	1.4	1.8	...
2008–2018	4.7	1.9	2.3	6.2	...

Source: World Bank (2021) and IMF (2021).

between the two periods stems not only from their quantitative evolution but also from the change in macroeconomic policy from *neoclassical orthodoxy* to *neoclassical Keynesianism*[2] that pretends to achieve full employment using only low-interest policy and an erratic expansionary fiscal policy, while keeping the *structural pillars* of the real economy-finance-labor nexus intact, particularly in HICs.

Keynes (1964 [1936]) suggested the socialization of financial investment to achieve full employment first by determining an optimum rate of interest rate and second by achieving an equal distribution of income because full employment depends on aggregate demand, and aggregate demand depends on the equal distribution of aggregate income between capital and labor. Policy interest is a policy tool to adjust savings and investment, and the optimal (real) interest rate is a means of the socialization of finance capital to stimulate both production and consumption (Keynes, 1964 [1936]: 378). However, if aggregate income is not distributed equally between capital and labor, a steady increase in aggregate output cannot be achieved (Cingano, 2014: for an extensive review of inequality-growth nexus, see Cingano, 2014; OECD, 2014). In other words, the imposition of low real interest rates can ensure the socialization of capital of any kind in a *sustainable* manner only when complemented or accommodated by a declining inequality of income (Keynes, 1964 [1936]: 377). Otherwise, it will remain a policy tool to make adjustments between macro- and micro-financial balances, a process throughout which the negative externalities of finance cannot be expected to turn positive (as the evidence in this book demonstrates).

Given these basic theoretical-practical insights, the Great Recession of 2008–2009 and the ensuing Secular Stagnation of 2010–2021 turned out to be the periods of *reorganizational crisis*, specifically in terms of the real economy-finance-labor nexus. The enduring crisis draws on a fundamental policy trap between (i) the necessity of structural transformations such as the adaptation of redistributive macro and micro incomes policy by progressive taxation and efficiency wages, respectively, *and* the in-built institutional rigidities of finance capitalism that preclude the initiation of these transformations; (ii) the requirements of achieving economic resilience by monetary expansion due to the lack of a real increase in the household income *and* monetary policy normalization due to its structural risks, such as causing debt overhang, lower demand, and increasing inflation and financial fragility[3] (Karadi & Nakov, 2021); (iii) the ever-increasing leverage levels in the balance sheets of real economic actors (IMF, 2018) *and* the necessity of steadily increasing aggregate demand to achieve full employment on sustainable pillars; and (iv) the stagnant or uneven increase in labor's share of aggregate income (ILO & OECD, 2015) *and* the necessity of increasing this share strongly and steadily as a major driver of aggregate demand. The effect of this trap on the real economy-finance-labor nexus is a matter of empirical analysis, which will be conducted in the next section.

2.2.1 Complementarities and Financialization

The theory of complementarity can be utilized to conceptualize the complex interactions between real economy, finance, and labor. Complementarities (CMTs) are defined as the mutual reinforcement among a certain group of institutions in part or all of a social structure that improves or worsens clustering relative to alternative configurations. This is a revised definition of that made by Hall and Soskice (2001) that includes two things: CMTs may be both positive and negative, and they can both improve and worsen clustering.

There are mainly two types of CMTs. The first is synergy, which emerges when there is mutual reinforcement between two or more variables to achieve a certain purpose. The second type is supplementarity, in which one institution makes up for the deficiencies of the others, such as the offsetting of the vicissitudes of a highly liberalized labor market through strong familial support (Deeg, 2007). Our analysis prioritizes synergy due to its analytic scope.

There are five types of potential CMTs of the synergy kind between real economy, AFND-FMD-FOD, and compensation of employees, shown in Table 2.2 and Figure 2.1: (1) between the components of real economy themselves in stimulating or de-stimulating AFND, FMD, and FOD, illustrated by the arrow numbered 1 in Figure 2.1; (2) between AFND, FMD, and FOD in stimulating or de-stimulating the components of real economy, arrow numbered 3 in Figure 2.1; (3) between the components of real economy in stimulating or de-stimulating compensation of employees, arrow numbered 2;

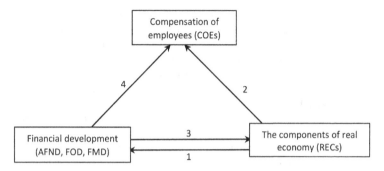

Figure 2.1 Complementarities between RECs, FND, and COEs.

(4) between AFND, FMD, and FOD in stimulating or de-stimulating compensation of employees, arrow numbered 4, and (ii) between the components of real economy and one, two, or all of AFND, FMD, and FOD in stimulating or de-stimulating compensation of employees, arrows numbered 2 and 4.

When there is a negative or positive synergy or mutual reinforcement between a sufficient number of variables in creating a joint effect, we title those CMTs that underlay these effects as NCMTs and PCMTs. This distinction is necessary to ascertain the partial or overall relationships between the variables. However, some effects of two or more variables on the other(s) might be positive, whereas the others are negative. For example, few components of real economy may cause a negative effect on the compensation of employees, while the rest cause a positive effect. Two effects of AFND, FOD, and FMD would stimulate real economic activity while the others do not. In conceptualizing these diverging or converging trends, we suggest two modes of governance: systemic and fragmented.

Systemic governance of the real economy-finance-labor nexus can be defined as a process of decision-making, regulation, or monitoring that aims to manage the nexus in a way to create NCMTs or PCMTs between real economy, finance, and compensation of employees. *Systemic* governance matters because five types of CMTs take effect through the majority of the components of real economy and AFND-FMD-FOD. The fragmented governance of the real economy-finance-labor nexus emerges when the nexus is managed in a way not to create either NCMTs or PCMTs. Fragmentation means that there is no synergy between the majority of the components of real economy in stimulating or de-stimulating FND or compensation of employees, nor between AFND, FMD, and FOD in stimulating or de-stimulating real economic activity or compensation of employees. Instead, the majority of the components of real economy either have diverse or no effects on AFND-FMD-FOD or compensation of employees, and AFND-FMD-FOD on real economic activity and compensation of employees. Diverse effects or no effects demonstrate the lack of complementary relationships between the components of real economy and AFND-FMD-FOD in achieving a certain purpose.

Notes

1 We do not take the Varieties of Capitalism thesis (VoC) as our reference point for three major reasons. First, VoC thesis takes a corporate-centered approach and is yet to be contextualized into a macroeconomic perspective (Scharpf, 2015). Second, VoC thesis neglected both similar commonalities and interdependencies of capitalism in terms of macro-institutional dynamics (Streeck, 2018). Interdependencies are significant for our period of study when commercial and financial systems were heavily deregulated. It is hence quite ambiguous if there is a variety of capitalism for the period of study in this book, 1980–2018, regarding macroeconomic and financial systems (Pontusson, 2005; Streeck, 2009). Even though certain institutional characteristics remain still diverse, we do not concentrate on micro-institutional characteristics (Tomaskovic-Devey & Lin, 2011) but macroeconomic structures that have been under the sway of neo-classical or neoliberal rule across the world, though at changing intensities, roughly from the 1980s onwards. Third, VoC thesis takes complementarities (CMTs) as unilaterally positive in a *static* manner and does not consider that they can be both negative or a mix of positive and negative in *dynamic* evolution. This is significant to make an analysis of the RECs-FND-COEs nexus, for example, regarding the potential negative CMTs between RECs and FND in de-stimulating COEs over a period when labor has been in defense against capitalist pressure.
2 Neo-classical Keynesianism differs from New Keynesianism or New Keynesian School of Economics in the sense the latter emerged out of the Keynesians' search for incorporating the influence of inflationary expectations and the impact of supply shocks into the orthodox Philips curve analysis (Snowdon & Vane, 2005: 357–432).
3 IMF (2018) argues that, under the guide of the Basel III criteria, global financial system has become safer, more resilient, less leveraged, more liquid, and better supervised. However, to the best of our knowledge, there is no work illustrating that the finance sector has started serving growth or labor. As a well-established fact, the sector's relative stability is thanks to the de-socialization of massive public funds and "infrastructural power" provided by monetary authorities by helping, establishing, expanding, and reviving financial markets as the durability and coherence of monetary policy in particular of quantitative easing kind is possible only with excessive financial growth (Braun, 2020; Walter & Wansleben, 2020).

References

Beck, T. 2012. Finance and growth–lessons from the literature and the recent crisis. *LSE Growth Commission, 3*, 1–6.

Braun, B. 2020. Central banking and the infrastructural power of finance: The case of ECB support for repo and securitization markets. *Socio-Economic Review, 18*(2), 395–418.

Cingano, F. 2014. *Trends in income inequality and its impact on economic growth.* OECD, Paris.

Deeg, R. 2007. Complementarity and institutional change in capitalist systems. *Journal of European Public Policy, 14*(4), 611–630.

Epstein, G. A. 2005. *Financialization and the world economy.* Edward Elgar Publishing, Cheltenham.

Hall, P. A., and Soskice, D. 2001. *The institutional foundations of comparative advantage*. New York, NY, Oxford University Press.

ILO, and OECD. 2015. Income inequality and labour income share in G20 countries: Trends, impacts and causes. Prepared for the G20 Labour and Employment Ministers Meeting and Joint Meeting with the G20 Finance Ministers, Ankara, Turkey, 3–4 September 2015. ILO, Geneva.

IMF. 2021. *Financial development database*. IMF, Washington, DC.

IMF. (2018). *World economic outlook*. IMF, Washington, DC.

Karadi, P., and Nakov, A. 2021. Effectiveness and addictiveness of quantitative easing. *Journal of Monetary Economics, 117*, 1096–1117.

Keynes, J. M. 1964. *The general theory of employment, interest, and money*. First Harbinger Edition. Harcourt Brace Jovanovich, New York and London.

Krippner, G. R. 2005. The financialization of the American economy. *Socio-Economic Review, 3*(2), 173–208.

OECD. 2014. *Does income inequality hurt economic growth? Focus on inequality and growth*. OECD Publishing, Paris.

Pontusson, J. 2005. Varieties and commonalities of capitalism. In *Varieties of capitalism, varieties of approaches* (pp. 163–188). New York: Springer.

Scharpf, F. W. 2015. Is there a successful "German model"? In *The German model: Seen by its neighbours* (pp. 87–103). SE Publishing.

Snowdon, B., and Vane, H. R. (2005). *Modern macroeconomics: Its origins, development and current*.

Streeck, W. (2009). *Re-forming capitalism: Institutional change in the German political economy*. Oxford University Press, Oxford.

Streeck, W. 2018. E Pluribus Unum? Varieties and commonalities of capitalism. In *The sociology of economic life* (pp. 419–455). Routledge, London.

Tomaskovic-Devey, D., and Lin, K.-H. 2011. Income dynamics, economic rents, and the financialization of the US economy. *American Sociological Review, 76*(4), 538–559.

Van der Zwan, N. 2014. Making sense of financialization. *Socio-Economic Review, 12*(1), 99–129.

Walter, T., and Wansleben, L. 2020. How central bankers learned to love financialization: The fed, the bank, and the enlisting of unfettered markets in the conduct of monetary policy. *Socio-Economic Review, 18*(3), 625–653.

World Bank. 2021. *World development indicators*. World Bank, Washington, DC.

3 Measuring Financialization

3.1 How to Measure Financialization?

We estimate multivariate and causal relationships between real economy, finance, and labor by the Panel Vector Autoregression (PVAR) model and the Panel Granger Causality test, respectively. PVAR measures correlations between the variables for a certain period of time. The PVAR modeling approach combines the traditional VAR approach, which treats all variables in the system endogenously, with the panel dataset, thereby allowing unobserved individual heterogeneity (Love & Zicchino, 2006). Using Ordinary Least Squares (OLS) in estimating Eq. (A3.1) would lead to inconsistent and biased results, as the unobserved panel fixed effect is correlated with the lag of the independent variables (Arellano & Bond, 1991). We use the generalized method of moments (GMM) estimator to estimate PVAR models because it uses the lag of the dependent variable as an instrument to obtain consistent and efficient estimates under this condition (Arellano & Bond, 1991). The technical details of the PVAR methodology are presented as an appendix (Appendix 3) to this chapter.

For the estimations of PVAR models to be stable and their results to be robust, all eigenvalues of the models should lie in the unit circle.[1] A precondition for this stability is that all the companion matrices should be strictly less than one.[2] If statistically significant and stable, positive correlation refers to a case, respectively, when one variable increases, the other also increases. Negative correlation refers to a case when one variable increases and the other decreases. We have three periods of analysis: 1980–2018, 1980–2007 and 2008–2018. We prefer PVAR because, first, it works for both large and small T, which is the case for the first two and the last period, respectively (In our case, the period 2008–2018 is too short for running a panel cointegration test of any kind). Second, it allows estimating relationships between two or more variables, which is significant in estimating bilateral relationships between all components of real economic activity (*recs*) and one of aggregate financial development (*afnd*), financial market development (*fmd*), or financial organizational development (*fod*) in a single model.

DOI: 10.4324/9781003336105-4

Correlation measures relationships but not causality. In other words, correlation does not illustrate that a change in the value of one variable is due to a change in the value of the other variable. Panel Granger Causality estimates unidirectional or bidirectional causality between two or more variables in a multivariate setting. We use both PVAR and PVAR Granger Causality because, in our analysis, we need to illustrate both the causal relationships and the direction of these causal relationships in order to establish that the change in any of the *rec*s, financial development (*fnd*), or compensation of employees (*coes*) is due to a change in one or two of them. Underlying this is that complementarity rests upon mutual "reinforcement" effects between two or more variables in achieving a certain purpose, which can be illustrated by causal relationships. In other words, if there is a correlation but not causation, we cannot decide whether complementarity exists or not. Thus, Granger causality will illustrate the existence or the lack of complementarity, and the correlation coefficients will enable us to establish whether the complementarity is negative or positive through the signs of the correlation coefficients.

As illustrated in Tables 3.1 and 3.2, we set up three major models for PVAR and Panel Granger Causality estimations given the potential complementary relationships between *rec*s, *fnd*, and *coes*. Table 3.1 illustrates which nexuses and complementarities (CMTs) or synergies are estimated by which model. Table 3.2 illustrates the specification of the three major models and their variations to be estimated. Table 3.3 documents the definitions of all variables included in the three models. In addition to *rec*s, we also include total factor productivity (*tfp*) and inflation as control variables in the models. The inclusion of *tfp* lies in two points: the first is that the *coes* may decline due to the transformation of economic structures into more productive or capital-intensive sectors (ILO & OECD, 2015), and the second is that *tfp* is a key driver of long-run *rec*s. Inflation is included as an indicator of macroeconomic stability, which can have significant effects on both *fnd* and *coes*.

Table 3.1 The Complementarities to Be Estimated.

CMTs	Synergy between	Arrows At Figure	In jointly increasing or decreasing	To be estimated by	To be estimated for
1	*rec*s	1	*afnd, fod*, or *fmd*	Model 1	HICs; UMICs; LMICs
2	*afnd, fod*, and *fmd*	3	*rec*s	Model 1	HICs; UMICs; LMICs
3	*rec*s	2	*coes*	Model 2	HICs
4	*afnd, fod*, and *fmd*	4		Model 3	HICs
5	*rec*s and *fnd* (*afnd, fod, fmd*)	2 and 4		Models 2 and 3	HICs

Table 3.2 The Specification of Empirical Models.

Country groups $j = \begin{cases} 1, & for\ HICs \\ 2, & for\ UMICs \\ 3, & for\ LMICs \end{cases}$	Models $m_j = 1,\dots,M_j;$ $M_J = \begin{cases} 6, & for\ HICs \\ 3, & for\ UMICs \\ 3, & for\ LMICs \end{cases}$	Dimension of endogenously variable vector of PVAR models. $k_j = 1,\dots,K_j$	Equations of models*
1	$\mathbf{Y}_{11K_1,it} = (afnd_{it}, fdii_{it}, fdio_{it}, pcns_{it}, fcf_{it}, gexd_{it}, exp_{it}, imp_{it}, tfp_{it}, inf_{it})'$	10	1.1.1–1.1.10
	$\mathbf{Y}_{12K_1,it} = (fod_{it}, fdii_{it}, fdio_{it}, pcns_{it}, fcf_{it}, gexd_{it}, exp_{it}, imp_{it}, tfp_{it}, inf_{it})'$	10	1.2.1–1.2.10
	$\mathbf{Y}_{13K_1,it} = (fmd_{it}, fdii_{it}, fdio_{it}, pcns_{it}, fcf_{it}, gexd_{it}, exp_{it}, imp_{it}, tfp_{it}, inf_{it})'$	10	1.3.1–1.3.10
	$\mathbf{Y}_{14K_1,it} = (coe_{it}, fdii_{it}, fdio_{it}, pcns_{it}, fcf_{it}, gexd_{it}, exp_{it}, imp_{it}, tfp_{it}, inf_{it})'$	10	1.4.1–1.4.10
	$\mathbf{Y}_{15K_1,it} = (coe_{it}, afnd_{it}, tfp_{it}, inf_{it})'$	4	1.5.1–1.5.4
	$\mathbf{Y}_{16K_1,it} = (coe_{it}, fod_{it}, tfp_{it}, inf_{it})'$	4	1.6.1–1.6.4
	$\mathbf{Y}_{17K_1,it} = (coe_{it}, fmd_{it}, tfp_{it}, inf_{it})'$	4	1.7.1–1.7.4
2	$\mathbf{Y}_{11K_2,it} = (afnd_{it}, fdii_{it}, fdio_{it}, pcns_{it}, fcf_{it}, gexd_{it}, exp_{it}, imp_{it}, tfp_{it}, inf_{it})'$	10	2.1.1–2.1.10
	$\mathbf{Y}_{12K_2,it} = (fod_{it}, fdii_{it}, fdio_{it}, pcns_{it}, fcf_{it}, gexd_{it}, exp_{it}, imp_{it}, tfp_{it}, inf_{it})'$	10	2.2.1–2.2.10
	$\mathbf{Y}_{13K_2,it} = (fmd_{it}, fdii_{it}, fdio_{it}, pcns_{it}, fcf_{it}, gexd_{it}, exp_{it}, imp_{it}, tfp_{it}, inf_{it})'$	10	2.3.1–2.3.10
	$\mathbf{Y}_{11K_2,i\tau} = (afnd_{it}, fdii_{it}, fdio_{it}, pcns_{it}, fcf_{it}, gexd_{it}, exp_{it}, imp_{it}, inf_{it})'$ for $\tau = 2008,\dots, 2018.$**	8	2.4.1–2.4.8
	$\mathbf{Y}_{12K_2,i\tau} = (fod_{it}, fdii_{it}, pcns_{it}, fcf_{it}, gexd_{it}, exp_{it}, imp_{it}, inf_{it})'$ for $\tau = 2008,\dots, 2018.$***	8	2.5.1–2.5.8
	$\mathbf{Y}_{13K_2,i\tau} = (fmd_{it}, fdii_{it}, pcns_{it}, fcf_{it}, gexd_{it}, exp_{it}, imp_{it}, inf_{it})'$ for $\tau = 2008,\dots, 2018.$**	8	2.6.1–2.6.8

(*Continued*)

Table 3.2 (Continued)

Country groups $j = \begin{cases} 1, & \text{for HICs} \\ 2, & \text{for UMICs} \\ 3, & \text{for LMICs} \end{cases}$	Models $m_j = 1,...,M_j;$ $M_j = \begin{cases} 6, & \text{for HICs} \\ 3, & \text{for UMICs} \\ 3, & \text{for LMICs} \end{cases}$	Dimension of endogenously variable vector of PVAR models. $k_j = 1,...,K_j$	Equations of models*
3	$\mathbf{Y}_{11K_3,it} = (afmd_{it}, fdii_{it}, fdio_{it}, pcns_{it}, fcf_{it}, gexd_{it}, exp_{it}, imp_{it}, tfp_{it}, inf_{it})'$	10	3.1.1–3.1.10
	$\mathbf{Y}_{12K_3,it} = (fod_{it}, fdii_{it}, fdio_{it}, pcns_{it}, fcf_{it}, gexd_{it}, exp_{it}, imp_{it}, tfp_{it}, inf_{it})'$	10	3.2.1–3.2.10
	$\mathbf{Y}_{13K_3,it} = (fmd_{it}, fdii_{it}, fdio_{it}, pcns_{it}, fcf_{it}, gexd_{it}, exp_{it}, imp_{it}, tfp_{it}, inf_{it})'$	10	3.3.1–3.3.10
	$\mathbf{Y}_{11K_3,\tau t} = (afmd_{it}, fdii_{it}, pcns_{it}, fcf_{it}, gexd_{it}, exp_{it}, imp_{it}, inf_{it})'$ for $\tau = 2008,...,2018.$**	8	3.4.1–3.4.8
	$\mathbf{Y}_{12K_3,\tau t} = (fod_{it}, fdii_{it}, pcns_{it}, fcf_{it}, gexd_{it}, exp_{it}, imp_{it}, inf_{it})'$ for $\tau = 2008,...,2018.$**	8	3.5.1–2.5.8
	$\mathbf{Y}_{13K_3,\tau t} = (fmd_{it}, fdii_{it}, pcns_{it}, fcf_{it}, gexd_{it}, exp_{it}, imp_{it}, inf_{it})'$ for $\tau = 2008,...,2018.$**	8	3.6.1–3.6.8

Notes

$\mathbf{Y}_{jm_jk_j,it}$ denotes $K_j \times 1$ vector of observed random variables; $\boldsymbol{\alpha}_{m_j,i}$ is an $K_j \times 1$ vector of individual specific constants; $\boldsymbol{\varepsilon}_{jm_jk_j,it}$ is an $K_j \times 1$ vector of random variables that is independently and identically distributed over t with mean $\mathbf{0}$ and covariance matrix $\boldsymbol{\Omega}_{m_j}$; $\mathbf{A}_{m_j k_j}(\mathbf{L}) = I_{K_j} - \boldsymbol{\Phi}_{K_j,1}L - ... - \boldsymbol{\Phi}_{K_j,p}L^p$ is a pth order polynomial of the lag operator, $j = 1,2,3$, for HICs, UMICs, and LMICs, respectively; $m_j = 1,..., M_j$ denotes different model specifications; $k_j = 1,...,K_j$ is the number of endogenous variables; $\ell = 1,...,p$, $i = 1,...,N_j$, and $t = 1,...T$.

*The number of models is consistent with the specification given in each variable vector system in the PVAR system.

**Due to the limited number of observations in the time dimension only for the models to be estimated for the period 2008–2018, the number of parameters in models with 10 endogenous variables is too high for estimation. To be able to estimate these models, the variables *tfp and fdio* have been excluded from the models (There were no limits for the number of observations in the time dimension for the models to be estimated for the periods 1980–2018 and 1980–2007).

Table 3.3 List of Countries.

	HICs	UMICs	LMICs
1	Denmark	Botswana	Bolivia
2	Finland	Brazil	India
3	France	Costa Rica	Kenya
4	Germany	Fiji	Morocco
5	Iceland	Guatemala	Senegal
6	Italy	Malaysia	Sri Lanka
7	Korea, Rep.	South Africa	Tunisia
8	Norway	Thailand	
9	Spain		
10	Sweden		
11	United Kingdom		
12	United States		

Model 1 estimates the *recs*-*fnd* nexus, coded as *1.1*, *1.2*, and *1.3* in Table 3.2. We substitute *afnd* in *Model 1.1* with *fod* in *Model 1.2* and with *fmd* in *Model 1.3* (Thus, 1, 2, and 3 in *Models 1.1*, *1.2*, and *1.3* denote *afnd*, *fod*, and *fmd*, respectively). As Panel VAR and Panel Granger Causality tests give the results not only for unilateral effects of *afnd*-*fod*-*fmd* on *recs* but also of *recs* on *afnd*-*fod*-*fmd* in the same model, we will be able to establish bilateral relationships between *recs* and *afnd*-*fod*-*fmd* in *Models 1.1*, *1.2*, and *1.3*, respectively.

As illustrated in Table 3.2, *Models 1.1.1–1.1.10* estimate the bilateral relationships between *recs* and *afnd*, *Models 1.2.1–1.2.10* between *recs* and *fod*, and *Models 1.3.1 and 1.3.10* between *recs* and *fmd*. The third "1" in *Model 1.1.1* denotes that the first variable in this model—*fnd*—is the dependent variable. In a similar vein, "10" in *Model 1.1.10* denotes that the tenth variable in this model—*inf*—is the dependent variable. *1.1.1–1.1.10* denote that all models between 1.1.1 and 1.1.10 are estimated by using the same specification and only by changing the dependent variables in the way noted.

Model 2, coded as *1.4* in Table 3.2, estimates the effects of *recs* on *coes* (In this second model, we will also be able to establish the effects of *coes* on *recs*, but we are not interested in these effects in this book). Model 3, coded as *1.5*-*1.6*-*1.7* in Table 3.2, estimates the effects of *afnd*-*fod*-*fmd* on *coes*. *Model 1.5*, *Model 1.6*, and *Model 1.7* estimate the *afnd*-*coes*, *fmd*-*coes*, and *fod*-*coes* nexuses, respectively. *Models 1.5.1* and *1.5.2* denote that the first and second variables in these models, which are *coes* and *afnd*, respectively, are dependent variables. The same holds for *Models 1.6.1* and *1.7.1*.

In terms of CMTs, as illustrated in Table 3.1, Model 1 estimates CMTs between *afnd-fmd-fod* in stimulating or de-stimulating *recs* as well as between *recs* in stimulating or de-stimulating *afnd-fmd-fod*. Model 2 estimates CMTs between *recs* in stimulating or de-stimulating *coes*. Model 3 estimates CMTs between *afnd, fod,* and *fmd* in stimulating or de-stimulating *coes*. The results from Models 2 and 3 will demonstrate if there are CMTs between *recs* and *fnd* that jointly stimulate or de-stimulate *coes* at a certain period of time. Estimating all models will enable us to establish potential CMTs between *recs, afnd, fod, fnd,* and *coes*. Table 3.1 also illustrates which model to be estimated for high-income countries (HICs), upper-middle-income countries (UMICs), and lower-middle-income countries (LMICs). We are unable to estimate Models 2 and 3 for UMICs and LMICs due to the lack of consistent and sufficient observations of *coes* [Except World Development Indicators of the World Bank, we also looked into the other key databases such as ILOSTAT statistical database, World Income Inequality Database of the United Nations, and World Inequality Database].

Model 1, coded as *1.1, 1.2,* and *1.3* for HICs in Table 3.2, will be estimated using the same specifications for UMICs, and LMICs. *1.1, 1.2,* and *1.3* have been coded as *2.1, 2.2,* and *2.3* for UMICs, respectively, and *3.1., 3.2.* and *3.3* for LMICs, respectively. However, for the period 2008–2018, the number of parameters in these models was too high to be estimated due to the constraint of the limited number of observations in the time dimension. We had to leave two parameters from the specification of Model 1 so that we could estimate the models for this particular period, which are outward foreign direct investment (*fdio*) and total factor productivity (*tfp*), because *fdio* is a relatively less significant variable for developing economies and *tfp* as a control variable in our model is less significant than *inf,* which is a key determinant of not only *fnd* per se but also of the *recs-fnd* nexus (Ayadi et al., 2015; Kim & Lin, 2010). *Models 2.1, 2.2,* and *2.3* have been coded *2.4, 2.5,* and *2.6* after omitting *fdio* and *tfp* from their specifications. Similarly, *Models 3.1, 3.2,* and *3.3* have been recoded as *3.4, 3.5,* and *3.6,* respectively, after omitting *fdio* and *tfp* from their specifications.

The periods of estimation are 1980–2018, 1980–2007, and 2008–2018. We are unable to include the years 2019 and 2020 due to the lack of *afnd, fod,* and *fmd* data for these years at the time of writing. The periodization draws on the fact that the Great Recession started in December 2007 in the National Bureau of Economic Research (NBER's) estimation. In so doing, the periodization aims to find out if there are significant differences between the results of the periods before and after the Recession.

3.2 Financialization in High-Income, Upper-Middle-Income, and Lower-Middle-Income Countries

This section documents and discusses the empirical findings of the PVAR models using the GMM methods and of the Panel Granger Causality tests for HICs,

Table 3.4 The List of Variables and Data Sources.

Variable	Definition	Source
coe_{it}	Compensation of employees*	World Development Indicators (WDI)
$afnd_{it}$	Aggregate financial development	IMF Financial Development Database (FDD)
fod_{it}	Financial organizational development	IMF FDD
fmd_{it}	Financial market development	IMF FDD
$fdii_{it}$	Inward foreign direct investment*	WDI
$fdio_{it}$	Outward foreign direct investment*	WDI
$pcns_{it}$	Private consumption expenditures*	WDI
fcf_{it}	Fixed-capital investment*	WDI
$gexd_{it}$	Government consumption expenditures*	WDI
exp_{it}	Exports*	WDI
imp_{it}	Imports*	WDI
tfp_{it}	Total factor productivity	PENN World Tables
inf_{it}	Inflation (consumer prices)	WDI

Notes
Annual data between 1980 and 2018 ($T = 39$) for three different income groups.
*Percent of GDP.

UMICs, and LMICs, respectively. The list of countries can be seen in Table 3.4. As the number of PVAR models, PVAR stability plots, and PVAR Granger Causality tests are overly large, we document their results in Appendix 3.1, online Appendix 3.2, and Appendix 3.3, respectively (Appendix 3.2 is available on the website for the book). In the manuscript, we provide three Tables (Tables 3.5, 3.7, and 3.9) one for each country group, which demonstrate the results of both PVAR models for each country group. In these tables, one can see both the direction of correlation and of causality between the variables.

3.2.1   HICs

3.2.1.1   1980–2018

The results of the PVAR models, PVAR stability tests, and Granger causality tests for HICs have been documented in Tables A.1.1–A.1.2 in Appendix 3.1, Figures A.1.1–A.1.21 in online Appendix 3.2, and Tables A.1.1–A.1.3 in Appendix 3.3, respectively. All these results have been summarized in Tables 3.5 and 3.6. As Figures A.1.1–A.1.7 in online Appendix 3.2 demonstrate, all the models estimated for this period were stable.

Table 3.5 Panel VAR and Granger Causality Test Results for HICs.*

1980–2018

Variable	RECs → AFND	AFND → RECs	RECs → FOD	FOD → RECs	RECs → FMD	FMD → RECs	RECs → COEs
FCF	(+)	(−)	(n.a.)	(−)	(+)	(n.a.)	(+)
GEXD	(n.a.)	(n.a.)	(n.a.)	(n.a.)	(+)	(−)	(−)
EXP	(+)	(n.a.)	(n.a.)	(−)	(+)	(n.a.)	(+)
IMP	(−)	(n.a.)	(n.a.)	(−)	(−)	(n.a.)	(+)
FDII	(n.a.)	(+)	(+)	(+)	(n.a.)	(+)	(+)
FDIO	(n.a.)	(+)	(−)	(+)	(n.a.)	(+)	(+)
PCNS	(+)	(n.a.)	(n.a.)	(+)	(+)	(n.a.)	(−)
TFP	(−)	(−)	(n.a.)	(−)	(+)	(n.a.)	(+)
INF	(+)	(−)	(n.a.)	(+)	(+)	(n.a.)	(−)
ALL	(n.a.)	(n.a.)	(n.a.)	(−)	(n.a.)	(−)	

FND: AFND (−), FMD (−), FOD (−), ALL

1980–2007

Variable	RECs → AFND	AFND → RECs	RECs → FOD	FOD → RECs	RECs → FMD	FMD → RECs	RECs → COEs
FCF	(+)	(n.a.)	(+)	(−)	(+)	(n.a.)	(+)
GEXD	(+)	(n.a.)	(n.a.)	(n.a.)	(+)	(−)	(−)
EXP	(+)	(n.a.)	(+)	(n.a.)	(+)	(−)	(+)
IMP	(−)	(n.a.)	(−)	(+)	(+)	(+)	(+)
FDII	(n.a.)	(+)	(n.a.)	(+)	(+)	(+)	(n.a.)
FDIO	(+)	(+)	(n.a.)	(n.a.)	(+)	(+)	(n.a.)
PCNS	(n.a.)	(n.a.)	(+)	(n.a.)	(n.a.)	(n.a.)	
TFP	(−)	(−)	(+)	(−)	(+)	(n.a.)	(+)
INF	(−)	(−)	(n.a.)	(−)	(−)	(n.a.)	(−)
ALL			(n.a.)	(−)			

FND: AFND (−), FMD (−), FOD (−), ALL

(*Continued*)

Table 3.5 (Continued)

2008–2018

RECs →	AFND →	RECs →	FOD →	RECs →	FMD →	RECs →	COEs →	FND
FCF		FCF		FCF		FCF		
GEXD		GEXD		GEXD		GEXD		(–) AFND
EXP		EXP		EXP		EXP		
IMP		IMP		IMP		IMP		
FDII	AFND	FDII	FOD	FDII	FMD	FDII	COEs	(–) FMD
FDIO		FDIO		FDIO		FDIO		
PCNS		PCNS		PCNS		PCNS		
TFP		TFP		TFP		TFP		(–) FOD
INF		INF		INF		INF		
ALL		ALL		ALL		ALL		ALL

Notes

*This Table is based on Tables A.1.1–A.1.2 in Appendix 3, Figures between A.1.1 and A.1.21 in Appendix 4, and Tables between A.1.1 and A.1.3 in Appendix 5. Arrows denote the existence and direction of statistically significant Granger causal relationships.

Table 3.6 Complementarities and Financialization in HICs.*

CMTs	Between	PCMTs or NCMTs	on	Financialization
		1980–2018		
1	*recs*	PCMTs	*fmd*	Fundamental, regressive, and structural regarding *recs-fmd-coes* nexus; regressive financialization regarding *afnd-coes* and *fod-coes* nexuses
3	*recs*	NCMTs	*coes*	
4	*afnd, fod,* and *fmd*	NCMTs		
5	*recs* and *afnd, fod, fmd*	NCMTs		
		1980–2007		
1	*recs*	PCMTs	*afnd, fod, and fmd*	Fundamental, regressive, and structural regarding *recs-afnd-coes*; *recs-fod-coes*; and *recs-fmd-coes* nexuses
3	*recs*	NCMTs	*coes*	
4	*afnd, fod,* and *fmd*	NCMTs		
5	*recs* and *afnd, fod, fmd*	NCMTs		
		2008–2018		
4	*afnd, fod,* and *fmd*	NCMTs	*coes*	Regressive financialization regarding *afnd-coes*, *fod-coes*, and *fmd-coes* nexuses

Note

*The results of the periods 1980–2007 and 2008–2018 have been considered as there are stark differences between the results of these two sub-periods and those of the period 1980–2018 (see text for details).

As shown in Table 3.5, in the period 1980–2018, there is no convergence between the majority of *recs* in having a positive or negative effect on and Granger causing *afnd*, and *afnd* had no effect on and did not Granger-cause the majority of *recs*. Thus, we cannot conclude *fundamental financialization* in terms of the *recs-afnd* nexus for this particular period. Neither can we conclude fundamental financialization for the *recs-fod* nexus as the great majority of *recs* did not have any effect on and did not Granger-cause *fod*; likewise, *fod* had no negative or positive effects on and Granger-caused the majority of *recs*. However, the majority of *recs* in addition to *tfp* had positive effects on and Granger-caused *fmd*. In other words, there were positive complementarities (*PCMTs*) between *recs* in stimulating *fmd*. *fmd* had no effect on and did not Granger-cause the majority of *recs*. Thus, we can conclude *fundamental financialization* in terms of the *recs-fmd* nexus.

A great majority of *recs* and all of *afnd, fod,* and *fmd* had negative effects on and Granger-caused *coes*. In other words, there were negative complementarities (NCMTs) between *recs* themselves, between *afnd-fod-fmd* themselves, and thus between *recs* and *afnd-fod-fmd* in reducing *coes* in the period 1980–2018. Thus, we can conclude *regressive financialization* in terms of *fnd-coes* nexuses (*fnd* represents all of *afnd, fod,* and *fmd*).

Finally, we can conclude *structural financialization* originating in the *recs-fmd-coe*s nexus in this particular period, given that both fundamental and regressive financialization were present based on this nexus.

3.2.1.2   1980–2007

Figures A.1.8–A.1.14 in online Appendix 3.2 demonstrate that all the models estimated for this period were stable. As shown in Table 3.6 (based on Tables A.1.1–A.1.2 in Appendix 3.1 and Tables A.1.1–A.1.3 in Appendix 3.3), there were PCMTs between the majority of *recs* in having positive effects on and Granger-causing all of *afnd, fod,* and *fmd. afnd, fod,* and *fmd* had either no effect on and did not Granger-cause *recs* or they did not have an effect on or Granger-cause the majority of *recs* either in a positive or negative direction. In addition, there were NCMTs between the majority of *recs* and *tfp* as well as *afnd, fod,* and *fmd* in having negative effects on and Granger-causing *coes*. As a result, we can conclude *fundamental, regressive,* and thus *structural financialization* for all *recs-afnd-coe*s, *recs-fod-*coes, and *recs-fmd-coe*s nexuses for HICs in this particular period. A key point in this regard is that NCMTs between *recs* and *afnd-fmd-fod* demonstrate that *fnd*'s negative effect on *coes* occurs not only directly but also indirectly by the financialized structure of real economic governance.

Another point for this period is that there were negative causal effects running from *fmd* to government expenditures and exports and from *fod* to investment expenditures and imports. Even though this did not prevent the establishment of fundamental financialization for the *recs-fnd* nexus, these negative effects on the few *recs* can be suggested as providing additional support for the thesis of financialized economic governance in the period.

3.2.1.3   2008–2018

As Figures A.1.15–A.1.21 in online Appendix 3.2 demonstrate, *Models 1.1.1–1.1.10, 1.2.1–1.2.10, 1.3.1–1.3.10,* and *1.4.1.–1.4.10* were not stable in this period, which prevents us from interpreting their results. However, *Models 1.5.1–1.5.4, 1.6.1–1.6.4,* and *1.7.1–1.7.4* were stable. As Table 3.5 demonstrates (based on Tables A.1.1–A.1.2 in Appendix 3.1 and Tables A.1.1–A.1.3 in Appendix 3.3), there were NCMTs between *afnd, fod,* and *fmd* in terms of having negative effects on and Granger-causing *coes* negatively. As a result, for this period, we can conclude *regressive financialization* in terms of the *fnd-coe*s nexus.

3.2.2   *UMICs*

The results of PVAR models, PVAR stability tests, and Granger causality tests for UMICs have been presented in Tables A.2.1–A.2.2 in Appendix 3.1,

Table 3.7 Panel VAR and Granger Causality Test Results for UMICs.*

1980–2018

RECs → AFND → RECs	RECs→AFND	AFND(ANFD)→RECs	RECs→FOD	FOD→RECs	RECs→FMD	FMD→RECs
FCF	(–)	(–)	(–)	(–)	(n.a.)	(n.a.)
GEXD	(+)	(n.a.)	(+)	(+)	(+)	(n.a.)
EXP	(n.a.)	(n.a.)	(+)	(–)	(+)	(+)
IMP	(n.a.)	(–)	(–)	(–)	(–)	(+)
FDII	(+)	(n.a.)	(+)	(+)	(+)	(–)
FDIO	(n.a.)	(n.a.)	(n.a.)	(+)	(n.a.)	(n.a.)
PCNS	(n.a.)	(n.a.)	(–)	(n.a.)	(n.a.)	(n.a.)
TFP	(n.a.)	(–)	(+)	(–)	(n.a.)	(–)
INF	(n.a.)	(n.a.)	(+)	(–)	(–)	(n.a.)
ALL						

1980–2007

RECs → AFND → RECs	RECs→AFND	AFND(ANFD)→RECs	RECs→FOD	FOD→RECs	RECs→FMD	FMD→RECs
FCF	(–)	(–)	(–)	(–)	(–)	(–)
GEXD	(+)	(+)	(+)	(+)	(+)	(n.a.)
EXP	(–)	(n.a.)	(+)	(–)	(n.a.)	(n.a.)
IMP	(+)	(–)	(–)	(–)	(+)	(–)
FDII	(+)	(+)	(+)	(+)	(+)	(n.a.)
FDIO	(n.a.)	(+)	(n.a.)	(+)	(n.a.)	(n.a.)
PCNS	(–)	(–)	(n.a.)	(n.a.)	(–)	(–)
TFP	(–)	(–)	(+)	(–)	(–)	(–)
INF	(+)	(–)	(+)	(–)	(–)	(n.a.)
ALL						

Notes

*This Table is based on Tables A.2.1–A.2.2 in Appendix 3, Figures between A.2.1 and A.2.9 in Appendix 4, and Tables between A.2.1 and A.2.3 in Appendix 5. Arrows denote the existence and direction of statistically significant Granger causal relationships.

Figures A.2.1–A.2.9 in online Appendix 3.2, and Tables A.2.1–A.2.3 in online Appendix 3.2, respectively. These results have been summarized in Table 3.7.

As the cited Figures for the UMICs in online Appendix 3.2 illustrate, all models for the period 1980–2018 and 1980–2007 were stable. As Table 3.7 illustrates, for the period 1980–2018, the majority of *recs* had no complementary effects on *afnd, fod,* or *fmd,* either in a positive or negative direction. *afnd, fod,* and *fmd* had no effect on the majority of *recs,* either. Thus, we cannot conclude *fundamental financialization* for UMICs for the period 1980–2018. The same holds for the 1980–2007 period. As all the models were unstable in the period 2008–2018, as shown in Figures A.2.7–A.2.9 in online Appendix 3.2, we cannot interpret the results of either PVAR or the PVAR Granger causality tests. Overall, there were no clear-cut CMTs between *recs* and *afnd-fod-fmd,* indicating that the *recs-fnd* nexus was managed through a fragmented mode of governance.

However, there are some key micro CMTs between the variables. First, in the period 1980–2018, there were (i) bilateral negative effects and causation between *fcf* and *afnd-fod* and between *imp* and *fod*, and (ii) bilateral positive effects and causation between *gexd* and *fod*, between *fdii* and *fod*, and between *exp* and *fmd*. Second, in the period 1980–2007, there were bilateral negative effects and causation between *fcf* and *afnd*, *fod* and *fmd*, between *pcns* and *afnd - fmd*, and bilateral positive effects and causation between *gexd* and *afnd – fod* and between *fdii* and *afnd – fod*.

Overall, the significant results from these micro CMTs are, first, that there were micro NCMTs between investment expenditures and *afnd* and *fod* in both periods, indicating that nonfinancial businesses' demand for funds from the financial system and the financial system's supply of funds to nonfinancial businesses had a mutually weakening (reducing) trend. Second, there were micro PCMTs between government expenditures and *fod* as well as between inward foreign direct investment and *fod* in both periods, indicating that both governments and inward foreign direct investors' demand for funds from financial organizations, and the financial organizations' supply of these funds to both, had a mutually reinforcing (increasing) trend.

In addition to micro CMTs, one can also argue that there were fundamental *micro financializations* in terms of the criteria we have specified. Few *recs* had positive effects on or Granger-caused *fnd* components, whereas the latter had negative or no effects on and Granger-caused those *recs*, such as the relationships between government expenditures and *afnd-fmd*, inward foreign direct investment and *afnd-fmd*, and *EXP* and *fod* in the period 1980–2018. We suggest that these micro financializations are significant for further research and for developing policy alternatives to eliminate the negative externalities of financialization, but not enough to conclude *macro financialization* of the fundamental kind. As a corollary, one can conclude that there is micro financialization regarding the investment expenditures-*fnd* relationship as the financial system affects investment expenditures negatively. However, investment expenditures also affect *fnd* negatively. Thus, *fnd* does not dominate investment expenditures, which is the key prerequisite for determining financialization.

3.2.3 LMICs

The results of PVAR models, PVAR stability tests, and Granger causality tests for LMICs have been presented in Tables A.3.1–A.3.2 in Appendix 3.1, Figure A.3.1–A.3.9 in online Appendix 3.2, and Tables A.3.1–A.3.3 in online Appendix 3.2, respectively. These results have been summarized in Tables 3.8 and 3.9. As Table 3.8 illustrates, the majority of *recs* had positive effects on *afnd* and *fod*, whereas *afnd* and *fod* had no effects on the majority of *recs* in the period 1980–2018. Thus, we can conclude *fundamental financialization* in this period for *recs*-*afnd* and *recs*-*fod* nexuses. As for the period 1980–2007, the majority of *recs* had no joint effects on *afnd* and *fod* in a positive or negative direction but did have negative effects on *fmd*. *afnd*, *fmd*, and *fod* had no

Table 3.8 Panel VAR and Granger Causality Test Results for LMICs.*

1980–2018

RECs →AFND→ RECs			RECs →FOD→ RECs			RECs →FMD→ RECs		
FCF (+)	(+) FCF		FCF (+)	(n.a.) FCF		FCF (+)	(n.a.) FCF	
GEXD (+)	(n.a.) GEXD		GEXD (+)	(+) GEXD		GEXD (−)	(n.a.) GEXD	
EXP (+)	(n.a.) EXP		EXP (+)	(n.a.) EXP		EXP (+)	(n.a.) EXP	
IMP (−)	(n.a.) IMP		IMP (−)	(n.a.) IMP		IMP (−)	(n.a.) IMP	
FDII (n.a.)	(n.a.) FDII		FDII (n.a.)	(+) FDII		FDII (n.a.)	(n.a.) FDII	
FDIO (−) ANFD	(+) FDIO		FDIO (−) FOD	(+) FDIO		FDIO (−) FMD	(n.a.) FDIO	
PCNS (+)	(n.a.) PCNS		PCNS (+)	(n.a.) PCNS		PCNS (+)	(n.a.) PCNS	
TFP (n.a.)	(+) TFP		TFP (n.a.)	(+) TFP		TFP (+)	(n.a.) TFP	
INF (n.a.)	(n.a.) INF		INF (−)	(n.a.) INF		INF (n.a.)	(n.a.) INF	
ALL			ALL			ALL		

1980–2007

RECs →AFND→ RECs			RECs →FOD→ RECs			RECs →FMD→ RECs		
FCF (n.a.)	(n.a.) FCF		FCF (+)	(−) FCF		FCF (−)	(+) FCF	
GEXD (n.a.)	(+) GEXD		GEXD (n.a.)	(+) GEXD		GEXD (−)	(n.a.) GEXD	
EXP (n.a.)	(+) EXP		EXP (n.a.)	(n.a.) EXP		EXP (−)	(+) EXP	
IMP (n.a.)	(n.a.) IMP		IMP (n.a.)	(n.a.) IMP		IMP (+)	(+) IMP	
FDII (n.a.)	(+) FDII		FDII (n.a.)	(+) FDII		FDII (−)	(n.a.) FDII	
FDIO (n.a.) ANFD	(n.a.) FDIO		FDIO (n.a.) FOD	(+) FDIO		FDIO (+) FMD	(n.a.) FDIO	
PCNS (−)	(n.a.) PCNS		PCNS (n.a.)	(−) PCNS		PCNS (−)	(n.a.) PCNS	
TFP (+)	(n.a.) TFP		TFP (n.a.)	(−) TFP		TFP (−)	(+) TFP	
INF (−)	(−) INF		INF (−)	(n.a.) INF		INF (−)	(−) INF	
ALL			ALL			ALL		

Notes

*This Table is based on Tables A.3.1–A.3.2 in Appendix 3, Figures between A.3.1 and A.3.9 in Appendix 4, and Tables between A.3.1 and A.3.3 in Appendix 5. Arrows denote the existence and direction of statistically significant Granger causal relationships.

effects on the majority of *recs*. Thus, we can conclude no financialization in this particular period. There were also micro financializations in terms of the relationships between *FCF-EXP-PCNS* and *fmd* in the period 1980–2018; between *fdio-PCNS* and *fmd*; and between *FCF* and *fod* in the period 1980–2007 in addition to a micro PCMT between *IMP* and *fmd*.

Table 3.9 Complementarities and Financialization in LMICs

1980–2018				
CMTs	Between	PCMTs or NCMTs	on	Financialization
1	*recs*	PCMTs	*afnd* and *fmd*	Fundamental financialization regarding *recs-afnd* and *recs-fmd* nexuses
1980–2007				
1	*recs*	NCMTs	*fmd*	…

Appendix 3

We consider a K_j-variate homogeneous PVAR of order p with panel-specific fixed effects represented by the following system of linear equations,

$$\mathbf{Y}_{jm_jk_j,it} = \boldsymbol{\alpha}_{m_j,i} + \mathbf{A}_{m_jk_j}\left(\mathbf{L}\right)\mathbf{Y}_{jm_jk_j,it-\ell} + \boldsymbol{\varepsilon}_{jm_jk_j,it}, \tag{A3.1}$$

where $\mathbf{Y}_{jm_jk_j,it}$ denotes $K_j \times 1$ vector of observed random variables; $\boldsymbol{\alpha}_{m_j,i}$ is a $K_j \times 1$ vector of individual specific constants; $\boldsymbol{\varepsilon}_{jm_jk_j,it}$ is a $K_j \times 1$ vector of random variables that is independently and identically distributed over t with mean 0 and covariance matrix Ω_{m_j}; $\mathbf{A}_{m_jk_j}(\mathbf{L}) = \boldsymbol{I}_{K_j} - \boldsymbol{\Phi}_{K_j,1}L - \cdots \boldsymbol{\Phi}_{K_j,p}L^p$ is a p-th order polynomial of the lag operator; $j = 1, 2, 3$, for HICs, UMICs, and LMICs, respectively; $m_j = 1, \ldots, M_j$ is different model specifications; $k_j = 1, \ldots, K_j$ is the number of endogenous variables; $\ell = 1, \ldots p$, $i = 1, \ldots N_j$; and $t = 1, \ldots T$.

3.3 Panel VAR Granger Causality Test[3]

Let $\boldsymbol{x}_{it}$ be a m-dimensional vector of observed random endogenous variables for cross-sectional unit i at time t for $i = 1, \ldots, N$ and $t = 1, \ldots, T$. Suppose we stack the $\boldsymbol{x}_{it}$'s yields a K-dimensional vector $\boldsymbol{x}_t = (\boldsymbol{x}'_{1t}, \ldots, \boldsymbol{x}'_{Nt})'$ with $K = mN$ and it is generated by the following standard panel vector autoregression (PVAR):

$$\Phi(L)\boldsymbol{x}_t = \boldsymbol{c} + \boldsymbol{\varepsilon}_t, \tag{A3.2}$$

where $\Phi(L) = I_m - \Phi_1 L - \cdots - \Phi_p L^p$ is a p-th order polynomial of the lag operator L, $L^p \boldsymbol{x}_t = \boldsymbol{x}_{t-p}$, $\boldsymbol{c}$ is an $K \times 1$ vector of constants, and $\boldsymbol{\varepsilon}_t \sim IIDN(\boldsymbol{0}, \Sigma)$ is a Gaussian errors vector with variance-covariance matrix Σ of dimension $K \times K$.

Whether $\boldsymbol{x}_t$ contains unit roots or not, the time series property of $\boldsymbol{x}_t$ remain the same, is considered that are either equal to unity or fall outside the unit circle. If all roots of this equation fall outside the unit circle, the system is stable. Thus, Eq. (A3.1) can be estimated by Generalized Method of Moments (GMM).

$$\left|\Phi(\rho)\right| = \boldsymbol{0}. \tag{A3.3}$$

3.4 GMM Estimation

As proposed by Anderson and Hsiao (1982), the first difference transformation can be consistently estimated for all equations individually by instrumenting lagged differences with differences and levels of $\boldsymbol{x}_{it}$ from earlier periods. While the GMM approach leads to consistent estimates of PVAR, estimating Eq. (A3.1) as a system of equations may result in efficiency gains (Holtz-Eakin et al., 1988). By first differencing Eq. (A3.1):

$$\Delta x_t = \Phi\left(\Delta x_{t-1} - c\right) + \Delta \varepsilon_t, \tag{A3.4}$$

and the orthogonality conditions,

$$E\left[\Delta x_t - \Phi\left(\Delta x_{t-1} - c\right)\right] q_t' = 0, \tag{A3.5}$$

where

$$q_t = \left(1,\ x_{i0}',\ \ldots,\ x_{it-2}'\right)'. \tag{A3.6}$$

Stacking the $(T-1)$ in Eq. (A3.4) yields

$$X_i = Z_i \Lambda' + E_i, \tag{A3.7}$$

where $X_i = (\Delta x_2, \ldots, \Delta x_{t-2})'$, $Z_i = (X_{i,-1}, \iota_{T-1})$, ι_{T-1} be a $(T-1) \times 1$ vector of ones, $\Lambda = (\Phi, c)$, and $E_i = (\Delta \varepsilon_{i2}, \ldots, \Delta \varepsilon_{iT})'$. Premultiplying Eq. (A3.6) with $(mT/2 + 1)(T-1)$ block-diagonal instrumental variable matrix W_i yields

$$W_i X_i = W_i Z_i \Lambda' + W_i E_i. \tag{A3.8}$$

The hypothesis that all coefficients on the lag of variable Z_i are jointly zero in Eq. (A3.7) for variable m is used for Granger causality tests, as proposed by Abrigo and Love (2016). The test statistic is distributed as χ^2 under the assumptions of Eq. (A3.1).

Appendix 3.1 The Results of PVAR Model Estimations

Table A.1.1 Estimations of PVAR Models for HICS.

1980–2018

Model	Independent variables	Dependent variables fd_t	Model	Independent variables	Dependent variables coe_t
1.1.1			1.4.1		
	fd_{t-1}	0.408*		coe_{t-1}	0.486*
	$fdii_{t-1}$	0.018		$fdii_{t-1}$	−0.013*
	$fdio_{t-1}$	−0.014		$fdio_{t-1}$	0.016*
	$pcns_{t-1}$	3.041*		$pcns_{t-1}$	−1.075*
	inv_{t-1}	0.726*		inv_{t-1}	−0.085*
	$gcns_{t-1}$	0.244		$gcns_{t-1}$	−0.149*
	exp_{t-1}	2.152*		exp_{t-1}	−0.284*
	imp_{t-1}	−2.038*		imp_{t-1}	0.230*
	tfp_{t-1}	1.240*		tfp_{t-1}	−0.014**
	inf_{t-1}	−0.037		inf_{t-1}	−0.195*

1980–2007

Model	Independent variables	Dependent variables fd_t	Model	Independent variables	Dependent variables coe_t
1.1.1			1.4.1		
	fd_{t-1}	0.500*		coe_{t-1}	0.710*
	$fdii_{t-1}$	0.448*		$fdii_{t-1}$	0.028
	$fdio_{t-1}$	−0.002***		$fdio_{t-1}$	−0.018
	$pcns_{t-1}$	−0.789*		$pcns_{t-1}$	−1.300*
	inv_{t-1}	−0.199*		inv_{t-1}	−0.278*
	$gcns_{t-1}$	0.328*		$gcns_{t-1}$	−0.262*
	exp_{t-1}	−0.157***		exp_{t-1}	−0.443*
	imp_{t-1}	0.274*		imp_{t-1}	0.365*
	tfp_{t-1}	−0.289*		tfp_{t-1}	−0.020***
	inf_{t-1}	0.006**		inf_{t-1}	−0.304*

2008–2018

Model	Independent variables	Dependent variables fd_t	Model	Independent variables	Dependent variables coe_t
1.1.1			1.4.1.		
	fd_{t-1}	0.487*		coe_{t-1}	0.486*
	$fdii_{t-1}$	−0.105		$fdii_{t-1}$	−0.013*
	$fdio_{t-1}$	0.113		$fdio_{t-1}$	0.016*
	$pcns_{t-1}$	0.957*		$pcns_{t-1}$	−1.075*
	inv_{t-1}	3.368*		inv_{t-1}	−0.085*
	$gcns_{t-1}$	1.086*		$gcns_{t-1}$	−0.149*
	exp_{t-1}	1.555*		exp_{t-1}	−0.284*
	imp_{t-1}	−0.743*		imp_{t-1}	0.230*
	tfp_{t-1}	−10.220***		tfp_{t-1}	−0.014**
	inf_{t-1}	0.087*		inf_{t-1}	−0.195*

(Continued)

Table A.1.1 (Continued)

1980–2018

Model	Independent variables	Dependent variables fi_t	Model	Independent variables	Dependent variables coe_t
1.2.1	fi_{t-1}	0.672*	**1.5.1**	coe_{t-1}	0.066
	$fdii_{t-1}$	0.021*		fd_{t-1}	−0.041***
	$fdio_{t-1}$	−0.022**		inf_{t-1}	0.002
	$pcns_{t-1}$	−0.104		tfp_{t-1}	0.142*
	inv_{t-1}	−0.002			
	$gcns_{t-1}$	−0.100	**1.6.1**	coe_{t-1}	0.089
	exp_{t-1}	0.071		fi_{t-1}	−0.061*
	imp_{t-1}	−0.196***		inf_{t-1}	−0.001
	tfp_{t-1}	0.058		tfp_{t-1}	0.048
	inf_{t-1}	−0.021			

1980–2007

Model	Independent variables	Dependent variables fi_t	Model	Independent variables	Dependent variables coe_t
1.2.1	fi_{t-1}	0.570*	**1.5.1**	coe_{t-1}	0.073
	$fdii_{t-1}$	0.383*		fd_{t-1}	−0.041***
	$fdio_{t-1}$	0.001		inf_{t-1}	0.007
	$pcns_{t-1}$	−0.457*		tfp_{t-1}	0.095***
	inv_{t-1}	−0.168*			
	$gcns_{t-1}$	0.506*	**1.6.1**	coe_{t-1}	0.100
	exp_{t-1}	0.257*		fi_{t-1}	−0.070*
	imp_{t-1}	−0.182*		inf_{t-1}	−0.002
	tfp_{t-1}	0.455*		tfp_{t-1}	0.018
	inf_{t-1}	0.014*			

2008–2018

Model	Independent variables	Dependent variables fi_t	Model	Independent variables	Dependent variables coe_t
1.2.1	fi_{t-1}	−0.203	**1.5.1**	coe_{t-1}	0.356**
	$fdii_{t-1}$	−0.086		fd_{t-1}	−0.217*
	$fdio_{t-1}$	0.095		inf_{t-1}	0.000
	$pcns_{t-1}$	0.551		tfp_{t-1}	0.102
	inv_{t-1}	2.850			
	$gcns_{t-1}$	0.450	**1.6.1**	coe_{t-1}	0.586*
	exp_{t-1}	1.539		fi_{t-1}	−0.169**
	imp_{t-1}	−1.518		inf_{t-1}	0.012
	tfp_{t-1}	−7.089		tfp_{t-1}	0.064
	inf_{t-1}	−0.029			

(*Continued*)

Table A.1.1 (Continued)

1980–2018

Model	Independent variables	Dependent variables fm_t	Model	Independent variables	Dependent variables coe_t
1.3.1			1.7.1		
	fm_{t-1}	0.087		coe_{t-1}	0.149*
	$fdii_{t-1}$	−0.033		fm_{t-1}	−0.023*
	$fdio_{t-1}$	0.065		inf_{t-1}	0.006*
	$pcns_{t-1}$	11.798*		tfp_{t-1}	0.191*
	inv_{t-1}	3.696*			
	$gcns_{t-1}$	2.274*			
	exp_{t-1}	9.524*			
	imp_{t-1}	−8.503*			
	tfp_{t-1}	4.909*			
	inf_{t-1}	−0.126			

1980–2007

Model	Independent variables	Dependent variables fm_t	Model	Independent variables	Dependent variables coe_t
1.3.1			1.7.1		
	fm_{t-1}	0.054		coe_{t-1}	0.152*
	$fdii_{t-1}$	0.517*		fm_{t-1}	−0.018**
	$fdio_{t-1}$	0.001		inf_{t-1}	0.018**
	$pcns_{t-1}$	−2.114*		tfp_{t-1}	0.125*
	inv_{t-1}	−0.535*			
	$gcns_{t-1}$	0.267**			
	exp_{t-1}	−0.112			
	imp_{t-1}	0.348**			
	tfp_{t-1}	−0.406**			
	inf_{t-1}	−0.018*			

2008–2018

Model	Independent variables	Dependent variables fm_t	Model	Independent variables	Dependent variables coe_t
1.3.1			1.7.1		
	fm_{t-1}	1.066		coe_{t-1}	0.570**
	$fdii_{t-1}$	0.053		fm_{t-1}	−0.097**
	$fdio_{t-1}$	−0.058		inf_{t-1}	0.025
	$pcns_{t-1}$	0.578		tfp_{t-1}	−0.065
	inv_{t-1}	−0.017			
	$gcns_{t-1}$	−0.016			
	exp_{t-1}	0.129			
	imp_{t-1}	−0.012			
	tfp_{t-1}	0.399			
	inf_{t-1}	−0.005			

Note

*, **, and *** indicate significance at the 99%, 95%, and 90% confidence levels, respectively.

Table A.1.2 Estimations of PVAR Models for HICs Country Group.

		1980–2018					1980–2007					2008–2018		
Model	Dependent variables	Independent variables			Model	Dependent variables	Independent variables			Model	Dependent variables	Independent variables		
		fd	fi	fm			fd	fi	fm			fd	fi	fm
1.1.2	fdii	0.593*	-	-	1.1.2	fdii	0.065*	-	-	1.1.2	fdii	40.324	-	-
1.2.2	fdii	-	0.799*	-	1.2.2	fdii	-	0.047***	-	1.2.2	fdii	-	23.813	-
1.3.2	fdii			0.171**	1.3.2	fdii	-	-	0.024***	1.3.2	fdii	-	-	60.815
1.1.3	fdio	0.397*		-	1.1.3	fdio	0.060***	-	-	1.1.3	fdio	46.579	-	-
1.2.3	fdio	-	0.579*	-	1.2.3	fdio	-	0.025	-	1.2.3	fdio	-	18.229	-
1.3.3	fdio	-	-	0.126**	1.3.3	fdio	-	-	0.032***	1.3.3	fdio	-	-	40.731
1.1.4	pcns	0.007	-	-	1.1.4	pcns	0.011	-	-	1.1.4	pcns	-0.365	-	-
1.2.4	pcns	-	0.030**	-	1.2.4	pcns	-	0.007	-	1.2.4	pcns	-	-2.074	-
1.3.4	pcns	-	-	-0.002	1.3.4	pcns	-	-	0.000	1.3.4	pcns	-	-	-0.220
1.1.5	inv	-0.072**	-	-	1.1.5	inv	-0.016	-	-	1.1.5	inv	4.522	-	-
1.2.5	inv	-	-0.113*	-	1.2.5	inv	-	-0.056***	-	1.2.5	inv	-	0.619	-
1.3.5	inv	-	-	0.005	1.3.5	inv	-	-	0.020	1.3.5	inv	-	-	-0.745
1.1.6	gcns	-0.026*	-	-	1.1.6	gcns	-0.027	-	-	1.1.6	gcns	-2.225	-	-
1.2.6	gcns	-	0.024	-	1.2.6	gcns	-	-0.019	-	1.2.6	gcns	-	-2.872	-

(Continued)

Table A.1.2 (Continued)

		1980–2018					1980–2007					2008–2018		
Model	Dependent variables	Independent variables			Model	Dependent variables	Independent variables			Model	Dependent variables	Independent variables		
		fd	fi	fm			fd	fi	fm			fd	fi	fm
1.3.6	gcns	-	-	-0.015***	1.3.6	gcns	-	-	-0.017*	1.3.6	gcns	-	-	0.167
1.1.7	exp	0.010*	-	-	1.1.7	exp	-0.026	-	-	1.1.7	exp	-0.818	-	-
1.2.7	exp	-	-0.148*	-	1.2.7	exp	-	-0.063	-	1.2.7	exp	-	-1.572	-
1.3.7	exp			-0.014	1.3.7	exp	-	-	-0.041**	1.3.7	exp	-	-	0.840
1.1.8	imp	-0.033*	-	-	1.1.8	imp	0.003	-	-	1.1.8	imp	1.284	-	-
1.2.8	imp	-	-0.207*	-	1.2.8	imp	-	-0.088***	-	1.2.8	imp	-	-4.590	-
1.3.8	imp	-	-	-0.006	1.3.8	imp	-	-	-0.018	1.3.8	imp	-	-	0.035
1.1.9	tfp	-0.034**	-	-	1.1.9	tfp	-0.028*	-	-	1.1.9	tfp	2.511	-	-
1.2.9	tfp	-	-0.058*	-	1.2.9	tfp	-	-0.048*	-	1.2.9	tfp	-	1.156	-
1.3.9	tfp	-	-	-0.001	1.3.9	tfp	-	-	0.004	1.3.9	tfp	-	-	-0.550
1.1.10	inf	-0.706*	-	-	1.1.10	inf	-0.714*	-	-	1.1.10	inf	-2.590	-	-
1.2.10	inf	-	-0.963*	-	1.2.10	inf	-	-0.544**	-	1.2.10	inf	-	13.893	-
1.3.10	inf	-	-	-0.127*	1.3.10	inf	-	-	-0.145**	1.3.10	inf	-	-	3.974

Note

*, **, and *** indicate significance at the 99%, 95%, and 90% confidence levels, respectively.

Table A.2.1 Estimations of PVAR Models for UMICS.

	1980–2018			1980–2007			2008–2018	
Model	Independent variables	Dependent variables	Model	Independent variables	Dependent variables	Model	Independent variables	Dependent variables
		fd_t			fd_t			fd_t
2.1.1	fd_{t-1}	0.421*	**2.1.1**	fd_{t-1}	0.500*	**2.4.1**	fd_{t-1}	−1.533
	$fdii_{t-1}$	0.204*		$fdii_{t-1}$	0.448*		$fdii_{t-1}$	−2.643***
	$fdio_{t-1}$	−0.001		$fdio_{t-1}$	−0.002***		$pcns_{t-1}$	3.699***
	$pcns_{t-1}$	−0.369		$pcns_{t-1}$	−0.789*		inv_{t-1}	−0.774***
	inv_{t-1}	−0.137*		inv_{t-1}	−0.199*		$gcns_{t-1}$	−2.454***
	$gcns_{t-1}$	0.162**		$gcns_{t-1}$	0.328*		exp_{t-1}	−1.969
	exp_{t-1}	0.042		exp_{t-1}	−0.157**		imp_{t-1}	−1.019***
	imp_{t-1}	0.009		imp_{t-1}	0.274*		inf_{t-1}	0.341***
	tfp_{t-1}	0.040		tfp_{t-1}	−0.289*			
	inf_{t-1}	−0.002		inf_{t-1}	0.006**			

(Continued)

Table A.2.1 (Continued)

1980–2018

Model	Independent variables	Dependent variables fi_t
2.2.1		
	fi_{t-1}	0.551*
	$fdii_{t-1}$	0.258*
	$fdio_{t-1}$	0.000
	$pcns_{t-1}$	−0.411**
	inv_{t-1}	−0.111**
	$gcns_{t-1}$	0.216*
	exp_{t-1}	0.080
	imp_{t-1}	−0.006
	tfp_{t-1}	0.194**
	inf_{t-1}	0.009*

1980–2007

Model	Independent variables	Dependent variables fi_t
2.2.1		
	fi_{t-1}	0.570*
	$fdii_{t-1}$	0.383*
	$fdio_{t-1}$	0.001
	$pcns_{t-1}$	−0.457*
	inv_{t-1}	−0.168*
	$gcns_{t-1}$	0.506*
	exp_{t-1}	0.257*
	imp_{t-1}	−0.182*
	tfp_{t-1}	0.455*
	inf_{t-1}	0.014*

2008–2018

Model	Independent variables	Dependent variables fi_t
2.5.1		
	fi_{t-1}	−1.059
	$fdii_{t-1}$	−3.572
	$pcns_{t-1}$	2.195
	inv_{t-1}	0.121
	$gcns_{t-1}$	−4.588
	exp_{t-1}	−2.405
	imp_{t-1}	−1.558
	inf_{t-1}	0.339

(Continued)

Table A.2.1 (Continued)

	1980–2018			1980–2007			2008–2018		
Model	Independent variables	Dependent variables		Model	Independent variables	Dependent variables		Model	Independent variables	Dependent variables

Model	Independent variables	Dependent variables	Model	Independent variables	Dependent variables	Model	Independent variables	Dependent variables
2.3.1		fm_t	**2.3.1**		fm_t	**2.6.1**		fm_t
	fm_{t-1}	0.077		fm_{t-1}	0.054		fm_{t-1}	−0.757
	$fdii_{t-1}$	0.782*		$fdii_{t-1}$	0.517*		$fdii_{t-1}$	7.581
	fdi_{t-1}	−0.003		fdi_{t-1}	0.001		$pcns_{t-1}$	3.509
	$pcns_{t-1}$	−0.225		$pcns_{t-1}$	−2.114*		inv_{t-1}	−1.211
	inv_{t-1}	0.026		inv_{t-1}	−0.535*		$gcns_{t-1}$	9.317
	$gcns_{t-1}$	0.465*		$gcns_{t-1}$	0.267***		exp_{t-1}	3.315
	exp_{t-1}	0.688*		exp_{t-1}	−0.112		imp_{t-1}	0.748
	imp_{t-1}	−0.448*		imp_{t-1}	0.348**		inf_{t-1}	−0.216
	tfp_{t-1}	0.101		tfp_{t-1}	−0.406**			
	inf_{t-1}	−0.019*		inf_{t-1}	−0.018*			

Note

*, **, and *** indicate significance at the 99%, 95%, and 90% confidence levels, respectively.

Table A.2.2 Estimations of PVAR Models for UMICs Country Group.

	1980–2018					1980–2007					2008–2018			
Model	Dependent variables	fd	fi	fm	Model	Dependent variables	fd	fi	fm	Model	Dependent variables	fd	fi	fm
2.1.2	fdii	−0.008	-	-	**2.1.2**	fdii	0.117*	-	-	**2.4.2**	fdii	−0.891	-	-
2.2.2	fdii	-	−0.007	-	**2.2.2**	fdii	-	0.110*	-	**2.5.2**	fdii	-	−1.704	-
2.3.2	fdii	-	-	−0.030***	**2.3.2**	fdii	-	-	−0.025	**2.6.2**	fdii	-	-	0.353
2.1.3	fdio	1.577	-	-	**2.1.3**	fdio	5.233*	-	-	**2.4.3**	pcns	−3.041	-	-
2.2.3	fdio	-	0.939	-	**2.2.3**	fdio	-	3.783*	-	**2.5.3**	pcns	-	−2.021	-
2.3.3	fdio	-	-	−0.305	**2.3.3**	fdio	-	-	0.201	**2.6.3**	pcns	-	-	0.832
2.1.4	pcns	−0.019	-	-	**2.1.4**	pcns	−0.032*	-	-	**2.4.4**	inv	−8.952	-	-
2.2.4	pcns	-	0.025	-	**2.2.4**	pcns	-	0.003	-	**2.5.4**	inv	-	−4.763	-
2.3.4	pcns	-	-	0.007	**2.3.4**	pcns	-	-	−0.028*	**2.6.4**	inv	-	-	1.929
2.1.5	inv	−0.444*	-	-	**2.1.5**	inv	−0.361*	-	-	**2.4.5**	gcns	2.860	-	-
2.2.5	inv	-	−0.462*	-	**2.2.5**	inv	-	−0.230**	-	**2.5.5**	gcns	-	2.633	-
2.3.5	inv	-	-	−0.005	**2.3.5**	inv	-	-	−0.173*	**2.6.5**	gcns	-	-	−0.649
2.1.6	gcns	−0.004	-	-	**2.1.6**	gcns	0.208*	-	-	**2.4.6**	exp	1.206	-	-

(Continued)

Table A.2.2 (Continued)

1980–2018

Model	Dependent variables	Independent variables fd	fi	fm
2.2.6	gcns	-	0.116	-
2.3.6	gcns	-	-	−0.016
2.1.7	exp	0.067	-	-
2.2.7	exp	-	−0.054	-
2.3.7	exp	-	-	0.067**
2.1.8	imp	−0.244*	-	-
2.2.8	imp	-	−0.267*	-
2.3.8	imp	-	-	0.072
2.1.9	tfp	−0.150*	-	-
2.2.9	tfp	-	−0.139*	-
2.3.9	tfp	-	-	−0.028**
2.1.10	inf	−1.324	-	-
2.2.10	inf	-	−4.659*	-
2.3.10	inf	-	-	−0.577

1980–2007

Model	Dependent variables	Independent variables fd	fi	fm
2.2.6	gcns	-	0.314*	-
2.3.6	gcns	-	-	0.013
2.1.7	exp	−0.065	-	-
2.2.7	exp	-	−0.127***	-
2.3.7	exp	-	-	0.039
2.1.8	imp	−0.181*	-	-
2.2.8	imp	-	−0.121***	-
2.3.8	imp	-	-	−0.081**
2.1.9	tfp	−0.151*	-	-
2.2.9	tfp	-	−0.126*	-
2.3.9	tfp	-	-	−0.076*
2.1.10	inf	−8.450*	-	-
2.2.10	inf	-	−9.649*	-
2.3.10	inf	-	-	−0.816

2008–2018

Model	Dependent variables	Independent variables fd	fi	fm
2.5.6	exp	-	0.341	-
2.6.6	exp	-	-	−0.412
2.4.7	imp	−5.561	-	-
2.5.7	imp	-	−4.674	-
2.6.7	imp	-	-	1.633
2.4.8	inf	4.083	-	-
2.5.8	inf	-	2.727	-
2.6.8	inf	-	-	−1.367

Note

*, **, and *** indicate significance at the 99%, 95%, and 90% confidence levels, respectively.

Table A.3.1 Estimations of PVAR Models for LMICS.

1980–2018			1980–2007			2008–2018		
Model	Independent variables	Dependent variables	Model	Independent variables	Dependent variables	Model	Independent variables	Dependent variables
3.1.1		fd_t	**3.1.1**		fd_t	**3.4.1**		fd_t
	fd_{t-1}	0.534*		fd_{t-1}	0.300*		fd_{t-1}	0.712
	$fdii_{t-1}$	0.016		$fdii_{t-1}$	0.067		$fdii_{t-1}$	−0.241
	$fdio_{t-1}$	−0.005*		$fdio_{t-1}$	−0.002		$pcns_{t-1}$	0.155
	$pcns_{t-1}$	0.676*		$pcns_{t-1}$	−1.264***		inv_{t-1}	1.347
	inv_{t-1}	0.368*		inv_{t-1}	0.118		$gcns_{t-1}$	0.275
	$gcns_{t-1}$	0.156*		$gcns_{t-1}$	−0.010		exp_{t-1}	−0.104
	exp_{t-1}	0.378*		exp_{t-1}	−0.097		imp_{t-1}	−0.424
	imp_{t-1}	−0.331*		imp_{t-1}	0.051		inf_{t-1}	0.070
	tfp_{t-1}	−0.046		tfp_{t-1}	−0.417			
	inf_{t-1}	−0.049*		inf_{t-1}	−0.062*			

(Continued)

Table A.3.1 (Continued)

	1980–2018			1980–2007			2008–2018	
Model	Independent variables	Dependent variables	Model	Independent variables	Dependent variables	Model	Independent variables	Dependent variables
		fi_t			fi_t			fi_t
3.2.1	fi_{t-1}	0.622*	**3.2.1**	fi_{t-1}	0.495*	**3.5.1**	fi_{t-1}	0.363
	$fdii_{t-1}$	−0.054		$fdii_{t-1}$	−0.079		$fdii_{t-1}$	−0.953
	$fdio_{t-1}$	−0.004*		$fdio_{t-1}$	−0.001		$pcns_{t-1}$	−1.021
	$pcns_{t-1}$	0.366**		$pcns_{t-1}$	−0.908		inv_{t-1}	2.007
	inv_{t-1}	0.319*		inv_{t-1}	0.185*		$gcns_{t-1}$	0.119
	$gcns_{t-1}$	0.096***		$gcns_{t-1}$	−0.090		exp_{t-1}	−0.699
	exp_{t-1}	0.238*		exp_{t-1}	−0.179		imp_{t-1}	0.058
	imp_{t-1}	−0.181**		imp_{t-1}	0.125		inf_{t-1}	0.035
	tfp_{t-1}	−0.101		tfp_{t-1}	−0.062			
	inf_{t-1}	−0.048*		inf_{t-1}	−0.059*			

(Continued)

Table A.3.1 (Continued)

	1980–2018			1980–2007			2008–2018		
Model	Independent variables	Dependent variables	Model	Independent variables	Dependent variables	Model	Independent variables	Dependent variables
3.3.1		fm_t	**3.3.1**		fm_t	**3.6.1**		fm_t
	fm_{t-1}	−0.153		fm_{t-1}	0.176*		fm_{t-1}	19.499
	$fdii_{t-1}$	0.929		$fdii_{t-1}$	−1.133*		$fdii_{t-1}$	82.788
	fdi_{t-1}	−0.021*		fdi_{t-1}	0.009*		$pcns_{t-1}$	235.451
	$pcns_{t-1}$	3.497*		$pcns_{t-1}$	−6.244*		inv_{t-1}	89.570
	inv_{t-1}	2.445*		inv_{t-1}	−0.372***		$gcns_{t-1}$	23.828
	$gcns_{t-1}$	−0.503**		$gcns_{t-1}$	−0.833*		exp_{t-1}	50.719
	exp_{t-1}	2.227*		exp_{t-1}	−1.122*		imp_{t-1}	−85.947
	imp_{t-1}	−3.180*		imp_{t-1}	0.853*		inf_{t-1}	8.302
	tfp_{t-1}	1.394**		tfp_{t-1}	−1.967*			
	inf_{t-1}	0.015		inf_{t-1}	−0.085*			

Note

*, **, and *** indicate significance at the 99%, 95%, and 90% confidence levels, respectively.

Table A.3.2 Estimations of PVAR Models for LMICs Country Group.

1980–2018

Model	Dependent variables	Independent variables		
		fd	*fi*	*fm*
3.1.2	*fdii*	0.021	-	-
3.2.2	*fdii*	-	0.038***	-
3.3.2	*fdii*	-	-	-0.010
3.1.3	*fdio*	12.557*	-	-
3.2.3	*fdio*	-	14.728*	-
3.3.3	*fdio*	-	-	-0.023
3.1.4	*pcns*	0.002	-	-
3.2.4	*pcns*	-	-0.022	-
3.3.4	*pcns*	-	-	-0.009
3.1.5	*inv*	0.085***	-	-
3.2.5	*inv*	-	0.036	-
3.3.5	*inv*	-	-	-0.003
3.1.6	*gcns*	0.046	-	-
3.2.6	*gcns*	-	0.100***	-

1980–2007

Model	Dependent variables	Independent variables		
		fd	*fi*	*fm*
3.1.2	*fdii*	0.082*	-	-
3.2.2	*fdii*	-	0.129*	-
3.3.2	*fdii*	-	-	-0.031
3.1.3	*fdio*	5.500	-	-
3.2.3	*fdio*	-	12.186*	-
3.3.3	*fdio*	-	-	0.895
3.1.4	*pcns*	-0.034	-	-
3.2.4	*pcns*	-	-0.285**	-
3.3.4	*pcns*	-	-	-0.020
3.1.5	*inv*	-0.060	-	-
3.2.5	*inv*	-	-0.124***	-
3.3.5	*inv*	-	-	0.107*
3.1.6	*gcns*	0.131**	-	-
3.2.6	*gcns*	-	0.211*	-

2008–2018

Model	Dependent variables	Independent variables		
		fd	*fi*	*fm*
2.4.2	*fdii*	-0.832	-	-
2.5.2	*fdii*	-	-0.314	-
2.6.2	*fdii*	-	-	2.598
2.4.3	*pcns*	0.628	-	-
2.5.3	*pcns*	-	-0.022	-
2.6.3	*pcns*	-	-	-3.097
2.4.4	*inv*	-2.452	-	-
2.5.4	*inv*	-	-2.528	-
2.6.4	*inv*	-	-	3.211
2.4.5	*gcns*	0.067	-	-
2.5.5	*gcns*	-	0.311	-
2.6.5	*gcns*	-	-	2.673
2.4.6	*exp*	0.410	-	-
2.5.6	*exp*	-	0.799	-

(Continued)

Table A.3.2 (Continued)

Measuring Financialization 57

1980–2018

Model	Dependent variables	fd	fi	fm
3.3.6	gcns	-	-	0.022
3.1.7	exp	-0.037	-	-
3.2.7	exp	-	0.031	-
3.3.7	exp	-	-	0.017
3.1.8	imp	0.030	-	-
3.2.8	imp	-	0.027	-
3.3.8	imp	-	-	0.039
3.1.9	tfp	0.087*	-	-
3.2.9	tfp	-	0.084*	-
3.3.9	tfp	-	-	0.013
3.1.10	inf	-0.099	-	-
3.2.10	inf	-	-0.207	-
3.3.10	inf	-	-	-0.474

1980–2007

Model	Dependent variables	fd	fi	fm
3.3.6	gcns	-	-	0.038
3.1.7	exp	0.232**	-	-
3.2.7	exp	-	0.080	-
3.3.7	exp	-	-	0.129*
3.1.8	imp	0.121	-	-
3.2.8	imp	-	0.033	-
3.3.8	imp	-	-	0.217*
3.1.9	tfp	-0.039	-	-
3.2.9	tfp	-	-0.067*	-
3.3.9	tfp	-	-	0.034***
3.1.10	inf	-2.084*	-	-
3.2.10	inf	-	-0.609	-
3.3.10	inf	-	-	-1.318*

2008–2018

Model	Dependent variables	fd	fi	fm
2.6.6	exp	-	-	1.680
2.4.7	imp	-0.123	-	-
2.5.7	imp	-	-1.200	-
2.6.7	imp	-	-	-2.366
2.4.8	inf	-0.884	-	-
2.5.8	inf	-	-0.074	-
2.6.8	inf	-	-	3.348

Note

*, **, and *** indicate significance at the 99%, 95%, and 90% confidence levels, respectively.

Appendix 3.3   Panel Granger Causality Test Results

Table A.1.1 Panel Granger Results for HICS, 1980–2018.

Models		chi2	df	Prob
1.1.1	fd	2.35	1	0.13
	fdii	0.92	1	0.34
	fdio	36.71	1	0.00
	pcns	18.16	1	0.00
	inv	1.10	1	0.30
	gcns	50.88	1	0.00
	exp	55.65	1	0.00
	imp	16.51	1	0.00
	tfp	1.01	1	0.32
	inf	192.62	9	0.00
	ALL			
1.1.2	fdii	12.95	1	0.00
	fd	64.07	9	0.00
	ALL			
1.1.3	fdio	11.61	1	0.00
	fd	104.50	9	0.00
	ALL			

Models		chi2	df	Prob
1.2.1	fi	8.23	1	0.00
	fdii	5.48	1	0.02
	fdio	0.20	1	0.66
	pcns	0.00	1	0.98
	inv	0.60	1	0.44
	gcns	0.25	1	0.61
	exp	2.16	1	0.14
	imp	0.10	1	0.75
	tfp	2.19	1	0.14
	inf	117.76	9	0.00
	ALL			
1.2.2	fdii	13.75	1	0.00
	fi	93.86	9	0.00
	ALL			
1.2.3	fdio	11.65	1	0.00
	fi	149.33	9	0.00
	ALL			

Models		chi2	df	Prob
1.3.1	fm	0.91	1	0.34
	fdii	2.08	1	0.15
	fdio	39.62	1	0.00
	pcns	40.02	1	0.00
	inv	10.08	1	0.00
	gcns	72.14	1	0.00
	exp	71.68	1	0.00
	imp	22.24	1	0.00
	tfp	1.69	1	0.19
	inf	118.62	9	0.00
	ALL			
1.3.2	fdii	4.00	1	0.05
	fm	93.65	9	0.00
	ALL			
1.3.3	fdio	4.03	1	0.05
	fm	122.95	9	0.00
	ALL			

Models		chi2	df	Prob
1.4.1	coe	39.17	1	0.00
	fdii	33.02	1	0.00
	fdio	113.33	1	0.00
	pcns	8.85	1	0.00
	inv	10.37	1	0.00
	gcns	39.03	1	0.00
	exp	28.12	1	0.00
	imp	3.80	1	0.05
	tfp	9.83	1	0.00
	inf	250.73	9	0.00
	ALL			
1.5.1	coe	3.55	1	0.06
	fd	14.82	3	0.00
	ALL			
1.6.1	coe	7.22	1	0.01
	fi	8.26	3	0.04
	ALL			

(Continued)

Table A.1.1 (Continued)

Models

Models 1.1.x	coe	chi2	df	Prob
1.1.4	pcns			
	fd	0.49	1	0.48
	ALL	67.52	9	0.00
1.1.5	inv			
	fd	4.96	1	0.03
	ALL	195.78	9	0.00
1.1.6	gcns			
	fd	2.15	1	0.14
	ALL	97.83	9	0.00
1.1.7	exp			
	fd	0.06	1	0.81
	ALL	131.99	9	0.00
1.1.8	imp			
	fd	0.43	1	0.51
	ALL	158.08	9	0.00
1.1.9	tfp			
	fd	6.53	1	0.01
	ALL	167.72	9	0.00
1.1.10	inf			
	fd	18.60	1	0.00
	ALL	156.85	9	0.00

Models

Models 1.2.x	coe	chi2	df	Prob
1.2.4	pcns			
	fi	5.39	1	0.02
	ALL	60.06	9	0.00
1.2.5	inv			
	fi	12.96	1	0.00
	ALL	233.24	9	0.00
1.2.6	gcns			
	fi	1.47	1	0.23
	ALL	105.12	9	0.00
1.2.7	exp			
	fi	8.00	1	0.01
	ALL	141.34	9	0.00
1.2.8	imp			
	fi	12.41	1	0.00
	ALL	171.81	9	0.00
1.2.9	tfp			
	fi	11.94	1	0.00
	ALL	214.19	9	0.00
1.2.10	inf			
	fi	16.65	1	0.00
	ALL	184.70	9	0.00

Models 1.3.x	coe	chi2	df	Prob
1.3.4	pcns			
	fm	0.23	1	0.63
	ALL	81.66	9	0.00
1.3.5	inv			
	fm	0.12	1	0.73
	ALL	189.73	9	0.00
1.3.6	gcns			
	fm	2.88	1	0.09
	ALL	100.23	9	0.00
1.3.7	exp			
	fm	0.54	1	0.46
	ALL	141.19	9	0.00
1.3.8	imp			
	fm	0.07	1	0.79
	ALL	188.87	9	0.00
1.3.9	tfp			
	fm	0.04	1	0.84
	ALL	155.26	9	0.00
1.3.10	inf			
	fm	7.12	1	0.01
	ALL	195.56	9	0.00

Models

Models 1.7.1	coe	chi2	df	Prob
1.7.1	fm	7.94	1	0.01
	ALL	29.93	3	0.00

Table A.1.2 Panel Granger Results for HICS, 1980–2007.

Models (1.1.x / 1.2.x)

Models	1.1.1 — fd	chi2	df	Prob		Models	1.2.1 — fi	chi2	df	Prob
	fdii	23.74	1	0.00			fdii	22.47	1	0.00
	fdio	1.73	1	0.19			fdio	0.02	1	0.89
	pcns	26.83	1	0.00			pcns	11.87	1	0.00
	inv	10.29	1	0.00			inv	6.10	1	0.01
	gcns	3.59	1	0.06			gcns	0.03	1	0.86
	exp	32.34	1	0.00			exp	14.62	1	0.00
	imp	33.11	1	0.00			imp	19.67	1	0.00
	tfp	20.02	1	0.00			tfp	3.68	1	0.06
	inf	3.01	1	0.08			inf	1.15	1	0.29
	ALL	94.96	9	0.00			ALL	47.74	9	0.00
1.1.2	fdii	chi2	df	Prob		1.2.2	fdii	chi2	df	Prob
	fd	6.77	1	0.01			fi	3.79	1	0.05
	ALL	93.83	9	0.00			ALL	103.73	9	0.00
1.1.3	fdio	chi2	df	Prob		1.2.3	fdio	chi2	df	Prob
	fd	3.58	1	0.06			fi	0.63	1	0.43
	ALL	96.96	9	0.00			ALL	87.82	9	0.00

Models (1.3.x / 1.4–1.6.x)

Models	1.3.1 — fm	chi2	df	Prob		Models	1.4.1 — coe	chi2	df	Prob
	fdii	11.30	1	0.00			fdii	2.61	1	0.11
	fdio	8.00	1	0.01			fdio	0.91	1	0.34
	pcns	31.25	1	0.00			pcns	71.31	1	0.00
	inv	20.96	1	0.00			inv	31.16	1	0.00
	gcns	14.44	1	0.00			gcns	15.94	1	0.00
	exp	47.95	1	0.00			exp	37.43	1	0.00
	imp	41.93	1	0.00			imp	27.50	1	0.00
	tfp	22.23	1	0.00			tfp	2.90	1	0.09
	inf	3.73	1	0.05			inf	11.38	1	0.00
	ALL	108.96	9	0.00			ALL	110.69	9	0.00
1.3.2	fdii	chi2	df	Prob		1.5.1	coe	chi2	df	Prob
	fm	2.82	1	0.09			fd	3.81	1	0.05
	ALL	92.56	9	0.00			ALL	8.31	3	0.04
1.3.3	fdio	chi2	df	Prob		1.6.1	coe	chi2	df	Prob
	fm	3.31	1	0.07			fi	8.80	1	0.00
	ALL	85.82	9	0.00			ALL	9.21	3	0.03

(Continued)

Table A.1.2 (Continued)

Models

1.1.4	pcns	chi2	df	Prob
	fd	1.38	1	0.24
	ALL	118.52	9	0.00
1.1.5	inv	chi2	df	Prob
	fd	0.24	1	0.62
	ALL	143.35	9	0.00
1.1.6	gcns	chi2	df	Prob
	fd	2.32	1	0.13
	ALL	107.29	9	0.00
1.1.7	exp	chi2	df	Prob
	fd	0.48	1	0.49
	ALL	130.93	9	0.00
1.1.8	imp	chi2	df	Prob
	fd	0.00	1	0.95
	ALL	142.15	9	0.00
1.1.9	tfp	chi2	df	Prob
	fd	5.96	1	0.02
	ALL	112.13	9	0.00
1.1.10	inf	chi2	df	Prob
	fd	21.29	1	0.00
	ALL	158.56	9	0.00

Models

1.2.4	pcns	chi2	df	Prob
	fi	0.35	1	0.55
	ALL	108.08	9	0.00
1.2.5	inv	chi2	df	Prob
	fi	3.56	1	0.06
	ALL	158.23	9	0.00
1.2.6	gcns	chi2	df	Prob
	fi	0.72	1	0.40
	ALL	100.52	9	0.00
1.2.7	exp	chi2	df	Prob
	fi	2.23	1	0.14
	ALL	126.69	9	0.00
1.2.8	imp	chi2	df	Prob
	fi	2.88	1	0.09
	ALL	117.44	9	0.00
1.2.9	tfp	chi2	df	Prob
	fi	9.52	1	0.00
	ALL	115.32	9	0.00
1.2.10	inf	chi2	df	Prob
	fi	6.44	1	0.01
	ALL	107.14	9	0.00

Models

1.3.4	pcns	chi2	df	Prob
	fm	0.00	1	0.97
	ALL	124.65	9	0.00
1.3.5	inv	chi2	df	Prob
	fm	1.71	1	0.19
	ALL	121.46	9	0.00
1.3.6	gcns	chi2	df	Prob
	fm	3.92	1	0.05
	ALL	109.28	9	0.00
1.3.7	exp	chi2	df	Prob
	fm	6.12	1	0.01
	ALL	151.07	9	0.00
1.3.8	imp	chi2	df	Prob
	fm	0.89	1	0.35
	ALL	124.78	9	0.00
1.3.9	tfp	chi2	df	Prob
	fm	0.61	1	0.44
	ALL	92.05	9	0.00
1.3.10	inf	chi2	df	Prob
	fm	5.03	1	0.03
	ALL	172.40	9	0.00

Models

1.7.1	coe	chi2	df	Prob
	fm	5.83	1	0.02
	ALL	16.44	3	0.00

Table A.1.3 Panel Granger Results for HICS, 2008–2018.

Models 1.1.1	fd	chi2	df	Prob	Models 1.2.1	fi	chi2	df	Prob	Models 1.3.1	fm	chi2	df	Prob	Models 1.4.	coe	chi2	df	Prob
	fdii	0.08	1	0.78		fdii	0.09	1	0.77		fdii	2.19	1	0.14		fdii	0.18	1	0.67
	fdio	0.08	1	0.78		fdio	0.08	1	0.78		fdio	1.16	1	0.28		fdio	0.14	1	0.71
	pcns	0.01	1	0.94		pcns	0.00	1	0.95		pcns	0.01	1	0.91		pcns	0.42	1	0.52
	inv	0.13	1	0.72		inv	0.17	1	0.68		inv	0.00	1	0.99		inv	0.00	1	0.96
	gcns	0.05	1	0.82		gcns	0.02	1	0.90		gcns	0.00	1	0.99		gcns	0.09	1	0.76
	exp	0.09	1	0.76		exp	0.08	1	0.78		exp	0.01	1	0.91		exp	0.06	1	0.80
	imp	0.05	1	0.83		imp	0.03	1	0.85		imp	0.00	1	0.99		imp	0.01	1	0.92
	tfp	0.10	1	0.76		tfp	0.11	1	0.74		tfp	0.07	1	0.79		tfp	0.04	1	0.84
	inf	0.01	1	0.92		inf	0.01	1	0.94		inf	0.00	1	0.98		inf	0.35	1	0.55
	ALL	8.88	9	0.45		ALL	4.38	9	0.89		ALL	8.42	9	0.49		ALL	4.59	9	0.87
1.1.2	fdii	chi2	df	Prob	1.2.2	fdii	chi2	df	Prob	1.3.2	fdii	chi2	df	Prob	1.5.1	coe	chi2	df	Prob
	fd	0.35	1	0.56		fi	0.06	1	0.81		fm	0.10	1	0.76		fd	12.52	1	0.00
	ALL	0.75	9	1.00		ALL	1.00	9	1.00		ALL	0.56	9	1.00		ALL	14.49	3	0.00
1.1.3	fdio	chi2	df	Prob	1.2.3	fdio	chi2	df	Prob	1.3.3	fdio	chi2	df	Prob	1.6.1	coe	chi2	df	Prob
	fd	0.45	1	0.50		fi	0.18	1	0.67		fm	0.10	1	0.75		fi	4.71	1	0.03
	ALL	1.05	9	1.00		ALL	2.60	9	0.98		ALL	0.85	9	1.00		ALL	6.93	3	0.07

(Continued)

Table A.1.3 (Continued)

Models

Model		chi2	df	Prob
1.1.4	pcns			
	fd	0.02	1	0.89
	ALL	0.92	9	1.00
1.1.5	inv			
	fd	0.21	1	0.65
	ALL	0.68	9	1.00
1.1.6	gcns			
	fd	0.25	1	0.62
	ALL	1.20	9	1.00
1.1.7	exp			
	fd	0.03	1	0.87
	ALL	2.36	9	0.98
1.1.8	imp			
	fd	0.03	1	0.87
	ALL	4.93	9	0.84
1.1.9	tfp			
	fd	0.25	1	0.62
	ALL	0.51	9	1.00
1.1.10	inf			
	fd	0.02	1	0.90
	ALL	2.52	9	0.98

Models

Model		chi2	df	Prob
1.2.4	pcns			
	fi	0.18	1	0.68
	ALL	1.39	9	1.00
1.2.5	inv			
	fi	0.00	1	0.99
	ALL	0.43	9	1.00
1.2.6	gcns			
	fi	0.06	1	0.82
	ALL	0.73	9	1.00
1.2.7	exp			
	fi	0.02	1	0.88
	ALL	2.90	9	0.97
1.2.8	imp			
	fi	0.10	1	0.76
	ALL	6.10	9	0.73
1.2.9	tfp			
	fi	0.01	1	0.94
	ALL	0.32	9	1.00
1.2.10	inf			
	fi	0.12	1	0.73
	ALL	1.30	9	1.00

Models

Model		chi2	df	Prob
1.3.4	pcns			
	fm	1.18	1	0.28
	ALL	7.81	9	0.55
1.3.5	inv			
	fm	0.03	1	0.86
	ALL	7.00	9	0.64
1.3.6	gcns			
	fm	0.01	1	0.94
	ALL	2.72	9	0.97
1.3.7	exp			
	fm	0.16	1	0.69
	ALL	1.75	9	1.00
1.3.8	imp			
	fm	0.00	1	0.99
	ALL	0.83	9	1.00
1.3.9	tfp			
	fm	0.04	1	0.85
	ALL	1.43	9	1.00
1.3.10	inf			
	fm	0.07	1	0.79
	ALL	0.39	9	1.00

Models

Model	coe	chi2	df	Prob
1.7.1	fm	5.10	1	0.02
	ALL	6.85	3	0.08

Table A.2.1 Panel Granger Results for UMICs, 1980–2018.

Models

2.1.1	fd	chi2	df	Prob
	fdii	8.63	1	0.00
	fdio	0.78	1	0.38
	pcns	2.61	1	0.11
	inv	7.35	1	0.01
	gcns	3.26	1	0.07
	exp	0.25	1	0.62
	imp	0.01	1	0.91
	tfp	0.16	1	0.69
	inf	1.83	1	0.18
	ALL	39.16	9	0.00
2.1.2	fdii	chi2	df	Prob
	fd	0.06	1	0.81
	ALL	195.48	9	0.00
2.1.3	fdio	chi2	df	Prob
	fd	2.27	1	0.13
	ALL	116.14	9	0.00

Models

2.2.1	fi	chi2	df	Prob
	fdii	13.78	1	0.00
	fdio	0.24	1	0.63
	pcns	3.99	1	0.05
	inv	6.35	1	0.01
	gcns	7.06	1	0.01
	exp	1.11	1	0.29
	imp	0.01	1	0.94
	tfp	5.68	1	0.02
	inf	31.18	1	0.00
	ALL	95.48	9	0.00
2.2.2	fdii	chi2	df	Prob
	fi	0.07	1	0.80
	ALL	180.07	9	0.00
2.2.3	fdio	chi2	df	Prob
	fi	0.56	1	0.46
	ALL	162.18	9	0.00

Models

2.3.1	fm	chi2	df	Prob
	fdii	13.78	1	0.00
	fdio	0.24	1	0.63
	pcns	3.99	1	0.05
	inv	6.35	1	0.01
	gcns	7.06	1	0.01
	exp	1.11	1	0.29
	imp	0.01	1	0.94
	tfp	5.68	1	0.02
	inf	31.18	1	0.00
	ALL	95.48	9	0.00
2.3.2	fdii	chi2	df	Prob
	fm	0.07	1	0.80
	ALL	180.07	9	0.00
2.3.3	fdio	chi2	df	Prob
	fm	0.56	1	0.46
	ALL	162.18	9	0.00

(Continued)

Measuring Financialization 65

Table A.2.1 (Continued)

Models

Model		chi2	df	Prob
2.1.4	pcns	chi2	df	Prob
	fd	0.74	1	0.39
	ALL	122.78	9	0.00
2.1.5	inv	chi2	df	Prob
	fd	31.04	1	0.00
	ALL	609.63	9	0.00
2.1.6	gcns	chi2	df	Prob
	fd	0.00	1	0.96
	ALL	125.51	9	0.00
2.1.7	exp	chi2	df	Prob
	fd	0.83	1	0.36
	ALL	170.30	9	0.00
2.1.8	imp	chi2	df	Prob
	fd	15.82	1	0.00
	ALL	125.07	9	0.00
2.1.9	tfp	chi2	df	Prob
	fd	17.71	1	0.00
	ALL	204.83	9	0.00
2.1.10	inf	chi2	df	Prob
	fd	0.53	1	0.47
	ALL	94.28	9	0.00

Models

Model		chi2	df	Prob
2.2.4	pcns	chi2	df	Prob
	fi	0.86	1	0.35
	ALL	114.31	9	0.00
2.2.5	inv	chi2	df	Prob
	fi	16.58	1	0.00
	ALL	457.46	9	0.00
2.2.6	gcns	chi2	df	Prob
	fi	2.15	1	0.14
	ALL	186.54	9	0.00
2.2.7	exp	chi2	df	Prob
	fi	0.54	1	0.46
	ALL	193.14	9	0.00
2.2.8	imp	chi2	df	Prob
	fi	10.16	1	0.00
	ALL	130.76	9	0.00
2.2.9	tfp	chi2	df	Prob
	fi	15.05	1	0.00
	ALL	203.45	9	0.00
2.2.10	inf	chi2	df	Prob
	fi	7.08	1	0.01
	ALL	121.79	9	0.00

Models

Model		chi2	df	Prob
2.3.4	pcns	chi2	df	Prob
	fm	0.86	1	0.35
	ALL	114.31	9	0.00
2.3.5	inv	chi2	df	Prob
	fm	16.58	1	0.00
	ALL	457.46	9	0.00
2.3.6	gcns	chi2	df	Prob
	fm	2.15	1	0.14
	ALL	186.54	9	0.00
2.3.7	exp	chi2	df	Prob
	fm	0.54	1	0.46
	ALL	193.14	9	0.00
2.3.8	imp	chi2	df	Prob
	fm	10.16	1	0.00
	ALL	130.76	9	0.00
2.3.9	tfp	chi2	df	Prob
	fm	15.05	1	0.00
	ALL	203.45	9	0.00
2.3.10	inf	chi2	df	Prob
	fm	7.08	1	0.01
	ALL	121.79	9	0.00

Table A.2.2 Panel Granger Results for UMICs, 1980–2007.

Models

2.1.1	*fd*	chi2	df	Prob
	fdii	37.68	1	0.00
	fdio	3.08	1	0.08
	pcns	6.94	1	0.01
	inv	13.83	1	0.00
	gcns	12.94	1	0.00
	exp	3.70	1	0.06
	imp	7.90	1	0.01
	tfp	7.83	1	0.01
	inf	6.16	1	0.01
	ALL	131.71	9	0.00
2.1.2	*fdii*			
	fd	15.71	1	0.00
	ALL	280.43	9	0.00
2.1.3	*fdio*			
	fd	22.58	1	0.00
	ALL	303.42	9	0.00
2.1.4	*pcns*			
	fd	2.72	1	0.10
	ALL	284.52	9	0.00

Models

2.2.1	*fi*	chi2	df	Prob
	fdii	47.18	1	0.00
	fdio	0.64	1	0.42
	pcns	6.98	1	0.01
	inv	14.18	1	0.00
	gcns	32.79	1	0.00
	exp	19.60	1	0.00
	imp	8.57	1	0.00
	tfp	25.42	1	0.00
	inf	84.42	1	0.00
	ALL	302.97	9	0.00
2.2.2	*fdii*			
	fi	11.85	1	0.00
	ALL	259.14	9	0.00
2.2.3	*fdio*			
	fi	8.46	1	0.00
	ALL	354.30	9	0.00
2.2.4	*pcns*			
	fi	0.02	1	0.90
	ALL	268.60	9	0.00

Models

2.3.1	*fm*	chi2	df	Prob
	fdii	22.03	1	0.00
	fdio	0.07	1	0.80
	pcns	28.12	1	0.00
	inv	38.46	1	0.00
	gcns	3.72	1	0.05
	exp	0.80	1	0.37
	imp	6.43	1	0.01
	tfp	4.97	1	0.03
	inf	31.79	1	0.00
	ALL	180.09	9	0.00
2.3.2	*fdii*			
	fm	0.86	1	0.35
	ALL	351.05	9	0.00
2.3.3	*fdio*			
	fm	0.07	1	0.80
	ALL	225.60	9	0.00
2.3.4	*pcns*			
	fm	9.08	1	0.00
	ALL	318.78	9	0.00

(*Continued*)

Table A.2.2 (Continued)

Models

2.1.x				
2.1.5	*inv*			
	fd	19.09	1	0.00
	ALL	676.11	9	0.00
2.1.6	*gcns*			
	fd	12.13	1	0.00
	ALL	192.85	9	0.00
2.1.7	*exp*			
	fd	0.86	1	0.35
	ALL	149.13	9	0.00
2.1.8	*imp*			
	fd	10.44	1	0.00
	ALL	269.07	9	0.00
2.1.9	*tfp*			
	fd	16.86	1	0.00
	ALL	238.25	9	0.00
2.1.10	*inf*			
	fd	27.78	1	0.00
	ALL	226.58	9	0.00

Models

2.2.x				
2.2.5	*inv*			
	fi	4.48	1	0.03
	ALL	470.89	9	0.00
2.2.6	*gcns*			
	fi	24.80	1	0.00
	ALL	191.75	9	0.00
2.2.7	*exp*			
	fi	3.66	1	0.06
	ALL	136.54	9	0.00
2.2.8	*imp*			
	fi	3.34	1	0.07
	ALL	292.97	9	0.00
2.2.9	*tfp*			
	fi	9.18	1	0.00
	ALL	225.61	9	0.00
2.2.10	*inf*			
	fi	39.32	1	0.00
	ALL	239.35	9	0.00

Models

2.3.x				
2.3.5	*inv*			
	fm	12.03	1	0.00
	ALL	356.96	9	0.00
2.3.6	*gcns*			
	fm	0.20	1	0.66
	ALL	201.74	9	0.00
2.3.7	*exp*			
	fm	1.04	1	0.31
	ALL	156.88	9	0.00
2.3.8	*imp*			
	fm	6.04	1	0.01
	ALL	320.47	9	0.00
2.3.9	*tfp*			
	fm	13.17	1	0.00
	ALL	481.78	9	0.00
2.3.10	*inf*			
	fm	0.84	1	0.36
	ALL	201.16	9	0.00

Table A.2.3 Panel Granger Results for UMICs, 2008–2018.

Models		chi2	df	Prob	Models		chi2	df	Prob	Models		chi2	df	Prob
2.4.1	fd				**2.5.1**	fi				**2.6.1**	fm			
	fdii	0.01	1	0.94		fdii	0.01	1	0.91		fdii	0.06	1	0.80
	pcns	0.01	1	0.93		pcns	0.01	1	0.94		pcns	0.01	1	0.94
	inv	0.01	1	0.93		inv	0.00	1	0.98		inv	0.01	1	0.94
	gcns	0.00	1	0.95		gcns	0.01	1	0.91		gcns	0.04	1	0.85
	exp	0.01	1	0.91		exp	0.02	1	0.90		exp	0.03	1	0.87
	imp	0.01	1	0.93		imp	0.01	1	0.92		imp	0.01	1	0.92
	inf	0.01	1	0.93		inf	0.01	1	0.92		inf	0.02	1	0.90
	ALL	0.05	7	1.00		ALL	0.04	7	1.00		ALL	0.38	7	1.00
2.4.2	fdii				**2.5.2**	fdii				**2.6.2**	fdii			
	fd	0.00	1	0.96		fi	0.08	1	0.78		fm	0.01	1	0.94
	ALL	0.22	7	1.00		ALL	1.30	7	0.99		ALL	0.19	7	1.00
2.4.3	pcns				**2.5.3**	pcns				**2.6.3**	pcns			
	fd	0.01	1	0.93		fi	0.01	1	0.93		fm	0.02	1	0.89
	ALL	0.06	7	1.00		ALL	0.11	7	1.00		ALL	0.19	7	1.00

(Continued)

Table A.2.3 (Continued)

Models		chi2	df	Prob
2.4.4	*inv*	chi2	df	Prob
	fd	0.01	1	0.94
	ALL	0.02	7	1.00
2.4.5	*gcns*	chi2	df	Prob
	fd	0.02	1	0.89
	ALL	0.34	7	1.00
2.4.6	*exp*	chi2	df	Prob
	fd	0.00	1	0.96
	ALL	0.39	7	1.00
2.4.7	*imp*	chi2	df	Prob
	fd	0.02	1	0.88
	ALL	0.22	7	1.00
2.4.8	*inf*	chi2	df	Prob
	imp	0.01	1	0.91
	ALL	0.58	7	1.00

Models		chi2	df	Prob
2.5.4	*inv*	chi2	df	Prob
	fi	0.00	1	0.95
	ALL	0.04	7	1.00
2.5.5	*gcns*	chi2	df	Prob
	fi	0.01	1	0.91
	ALL	0.20	7	1.00
2.5.6	*exp*	chi2	df	Prob
	fi	0.00	1	0.98
	ALL	1.10	7	0.99
2.5.7	*imp*	chi2	df	Prob
	fi	0.02	1	0.90
	ALL	0.20	7	1.00
2.5.8	*inf*	chi2	df	Prob
	imp	0.01	1	0.92
	ALL	0.86	7	1.00

Models		chi2	df	Prob
2.6.4	*inv*	chi2	df	Prob
	fm	0.01	1	0.92
	ALL	0.05	7	1.00
2.6.5	*gcns*	chi2	df	Prob
	fm	0.07	1	0.79
	ALL	3.03	7	0.88
2.6.6	*exp*	chi2	df	Prob
	fm	0.00	1	0.95
	ALL	0.51	7	1.00
2.6.7	*imp*	chi2	df	Prob
	fm	0.05	1	0.83
	ALL	0.88	7	1.00
2.6.8	*inf*	chi2	df	Prob
	fm	0.02	1	0.89
	ALL	0.56	7	1.00

Table A.3.1 Panel Granger Results for LMICs, 1980–2018.

Models	fd	chi2	df	Prob	Models	fi	chi2	df	Prob	Models	fm	chi2	df	Prob
3.1.1	fd				**3.2.1**	fi				**3.3.1**	fm			
	fdii	0.02	1	0.88		fdii	0.50	1	0.48		fdii	1.66	1	0.20
	fdio	11.56	1	0.00		fdio	14.31	1	0.00		fdio	8.91	1	0.00
	pcns	13.64	1	0.00		pcns	5.99	1	0.01		pcns	15.63	1	0.00
	inv	21.77	1	0.00		inv	19.98	1	0.00		inv	27.51	1	0.00
	gcns	10.55	1	0.00		gcns	2.87	1	0.09		gcns	4.16	1	0.04
	exp	19.57	1	0.00		exp	10.15	1	0.00		exp	27.67	1	0.00
	imp	11.97	1	0.00		imp	5.20	1	0.02		imp	37.22	1	0.00
	tfp	0.09	1	0.76		tfp	0.59	1	0.44		tfp	6.26	1	0.01
	inf	32.96	1	0.00		inf	28.63	1	0.00		inf	0.16	1	0.69
	ALL	76.56	9	0.00		ALL	68.30	9	0.00		ALL	56.03	9	0.00
3.1.2	fdii	0.97	1	0.32	**3.2.2**	fdii	2.92	1	0.09	**3.3.2**	fdii	1.10	1	0.29
	fd					fi					fm			
	ALL	36.56	9	0.00		ALL	40.28	9	0.00		ALL	101.51	9	0.00
3.1.3	fdio	10.61	1	0.00	**3.2.3**	fdio	16.96	1	0.00	**3.3.3**	fdio	0.00	1	0.97
	fd					fi					fm			
	ALL	74.18	9	0.00		ALL	84.24	9	0.00		ALL	47.54	9	0.00
3.1.4	pcns	0.01	1	0.93	**3.2.4**	pcns	0.84	1	0.36	**3.3.4**	pcns	0.79	1	0.37
	fd					fi					fm			
	ALL	27.80	9	0.00		ALL	29.34	9	0.00		ALL	12.72	9	0.18

(Continued)

Table A.3.1 (Continued)

Models		chi2	df	Prob
3.1.5	inv	chi2	df	Prob
	fd	2.84	1	0.09
	ALL	90.99	9	0.00
3.1.6	gcns	chi2	df	Prob
	fd	0.72	1	0.40
	ALL	67.11	9	0.00
3.1.7	exp	chi2	df	Prob
	fd	0.21	1	0.65
	ALL	101.56	9	0.00
3.1.8	imp	chi2	df	Prob
	fd	0.23	1	0.63
	ALL	134.01	9	0.00
3.1.9	tfp	chi2	df	Prob
	fd	7.53	1	0.01
	ALL	62.55	9	0.00
3.1.10	inf	chi2	df	Prob
	fd	0.02	1	0.89
	ALL	62.88	9	0.00

Models		chi2	df	Prob
3.2.5	inv	chi2	df	Prob
	fi	0.32	1	0.57
	ALL	98.16	9	0.00
3.2.6	gcns	chi2	df	Prob
	fi	2.77	1	0.10
	ALL	59.44	9	0.00
3.2.7	exp	chi2	df	Prob
	fi	0.12	1	0.73
	ALL	93.62	9	0.00
3.2.8	imp	chi2	df	Prob
	fi	0.17	1	0.68
	ALL	129.57	9	0.00
3.2.9	tfp	chi2	df	Prob
	fi	8.79	1	0.00
	ALL	62.94	9	0.00
3.2.10	inf	chi2	df	Prob
	fi	0.09	1	0.76
	ALL	56.94	9	0.00

Models		chi2	df	Prob
3.3.5	inv	chi2	df	Prob
	fm	0.01	1	0.93
	ALL	108.67	9	0.00
3.3.6	gcns	chi2	df	Prob
	fm	1.34	1	0.25
	ALL	71.64	9	0.00
3.3.7	exp	chi2	df	Prob
	fm	0.24	1	0.62
	ALL	103.41	9	0.00
3.3.8	imp	chi2	df	Prob
	fm	1.58	1	0.21
	ALL	157.46	9	0.00
3.3.9	tfp	chi2	df	Prob
	fm	1.57	1	0.21
	ALL	67.22	9	0.00
3.3.10	inf	chi2	df	Prob
	fm	2.58	1	0.11
	ALL	55.05	9	0.00

Table A.3.2 Panel Granger Results for LMICs, 1980–2007.

Models		chi2	df	Prob
3.4.1	*fd*			
	fdii	0.00	1	0.95
	pcns	0.00	1	0.99
	inv	0.03	1	0.87
	gcns	0.02	1	0.89
	exp	0.01	1	0.95
	imp	0.04	1	0.83
	inf	0.03	1	0.87
	ALL	5.06	7	0.65
3.4.2	*fdii*			
	fd	0.06	1	0.81
	ALL	0.23	7	1.00
3.4.3	*pcns*			
	fd	0.11	1	0.75
	ALL	1.09	7	0.99

Models		chi2	df	Prob
3.5.1	*fi*			
	fdii	0.13	1	0.72
	pcns	0.09	1	0.77
	inv	0.04	1	0.84
	gcns	0.01	1	0.91
	exp	0.04	1	0.85
	imp	0.00	1	0.97
	inf	0.02	1	0.90
	ALL	0.40	7	1.00
3.5.2	*fdii*			
	fi	0.15	1	0.70
	ALL	2.96	7	0.89
3.5.3	*pcns*			
	fi	0.00	1	0.99
	ALL	0.75	7	1.00

Models		chi2	df	Prob
3.6.1	*fm*			
	fdii	0.00	1	0.97
	pcns	0.00	1	0.97
	inv	0.00	1	0.97
	gcns	0.00	1	0.97
	exp	0.00	1	0.97
	imp	0.00	1	0.97
	inf	0.00	1	0.97
	ALL	0.01	7	1.00
3.6.2	*fdii*			
	fm	0.00	1	0.97
	ALL	0.01	7	1.00
3.6.3	*pcns*			
	fm	0.00	1	0.97
	ALL	0.01	7	1.00

(Continued)

Table A.3.2 (Continued)

Models		chi2	df	Prob	Models		chi2	df	Prob	Models		chi2	df	Prob
3.4.4	inv	chi2	df	Prob	**3.5.4**	inv	chi2	df	Prob	**3.6.4**	inv	chi2	df	Prob
	fd	0.02	1	0.89		fi	0.04	1	0.85		fm	0.00	1	0.98
	ALL	0.06	7	1.00		ALL	0.09	7	1.00		ALL	0.02	7	1.00
3.4.5	gcns	chi2	df	Prob	**3.5.5**	gcns	chi2	df	Prob	**3.6.5**	gcns	chi2	df	Prob
	fd	0.00	1	0.98		fi	0.02	1	0.90		fm	0.00	1	0.97
	ALL	5.11	7	0.65		ALL	3.79	7	0.80		ALL	0.05	7	1.00
3.4.6	exp	chi2	df	Prob	**3.5.6**	exp	chi2	df	Prob	**3.6.6**	exp	chi2	df	Prob
	fd	0.01	1	0.94		fi	0.02	1	0.89		fm	0.00	1	0.97
	ALL	1.63	7	0.98		ALL	0.80	7	1.00		ALL	0.10	7	1.00
3.4.7	imp	chi2	df	Prob	**3.5.7**	imp	chi2	df	Prob	**3.6.7**	imp	chi2	df	Prob
	fd	0.00	1	0.99		fi	0.02	1	0.88		fm	0.00	1	0.97
	ALL	0.56	7	1.00		ALL	0.25	7	1.00		ALL	0.07	7	1.00
3.4.8	inf	chi2	df	Prob	**3.5.8**	inf	chi2	df	Prob	**3.6.8**	inf	chi2	df	Prob
	imp	0.01	1	0.93		imp	0.00	1	0.99		fm	0.00	1	0.98
	ALL	2.34	7	0.94		ALL	2.70	7	0.91		ALL	0.15	7	1.00

Table A.3.3 Panel Granger Results for LMICs, 2008–2018.

Models					Models					Models				
3.1.1	*fd*	chi2	df	Prob	**3.2.1**	*fi*	chi2	df	Prob	**3.3.1**	*fm*	chi2	df	Prob
	fdii	0.14	1	0.71		*fdii*	0.75	1	0.39		*fdii*	27.29	1	0.00
	fdio	2.27	1	0.13		*fdio*	0.28	1	0.60		*fdio*	8.24	1	0.00
	pcns	3.35	1	0.07		*pcns*	2.14	1	0.14		*pcns*	99.48	1	0.00
	inv	2.47	1	0.12		*inv*	6.28	1	0.01		*inv*	3.27	1	0.07
	gcns	0.01	1	0.92		*gcns*	0.94	1	0.33		*gcns*	17.16	1	0.00
	exp	0.45	1	0.50		*exp*	2.12	1	0.15		*exp*	23.53	1	0.00
	imp	0.15	1	0.70		*imp*	1.30	1	0.25		*imp*	8.56	1	0.00
	tfp	2.06	1	0.15		*tfp*	0.07	1	0.80		*tfp*	27.19	1	0.00
	inf	50.76	1	0.00		*inf*	35.21	1	0.00		*inf*	25.16	1	0.00
	ALL	93.76	9	0.00		*ALL*	71.22	9	0.00		*ALL*	141.82	9	0.00
3.1.2	*fdii*	chi2	df	Prob	**3.2.2**	*fdii*	chi2	df	Prob	**3.3.2**	*fdii*	chi2	df	Prob
	fd	8.94	1	0.00		*fi*	17.13	1	0.00		*fm*	1.61	1	0.20
	ALL	52.28	9	0.00		*ALL*	83.07	9	0.00		*ALL*	20.15	9	0.02
3.1.3	*fdio*	chi2	df	Prob	**3.2.3**	*fdio*	chi2	df	Prob	**3.3.3**	*fdio*	chi2	df	Prob
	fd	2.58	1	0.11		*fi*	9.51	1	0.00		*fm*	0.18	1	0.67
	ALL	74.73	9	0.00		*ALL*	70.07	9	0.00		*ALL*	93.20	9	0.00

(*Continued*)

Table A.3.3 (Continued)

Models

Models		chi2	df	Prob
3.1.4	pcns	chi2	df	Prob
	fd	1.54	1	0.22
	ALL	30.80	9	0.00
3.1.5	inv	chi2	df	Prob
	fd	0.87	1	0.35
	ALL	246.20	9	0.00
3.1.6	gcns	chi2	df	Prob
	fd	4.69	1	0.03
	ALL	55.48	9	0.00
3.1.7	exp	chi2	df	Prob
	fd	4.29	1	0.04
	ALL	75.08	9	0.00
3.1.8	imp	chi2	df	Prob
	fd	1.76	1	0.19
	ALL	129.46	9	0.00
3.1.9	tfp	chi2	df	Prob
	fd	1.70	1	0.19
	ALL	40.92	9	0.00
3.1.10	inf	chi2	df	Prob
	fd	6.83	1	0.01
	ALL	72.79	9	0.00

Models

Models		chi2	df	Prob
3.2.4	pcns	chi2	df	Prob
	fi	6.32	1	0.01
	ALL	34.27	9	0.00
3.2.5	inv	chi2	df	Prob
	fi	3.62	1	0.06
	ALL	217.14	9	0.00
3.2.6	gcns	chi2	df	Prob
	fi	10.55	1	0.00
	ALL	60.03	9	0.00
3.2.7	exp	chi2	df	Prob
	fi	0.60	1	0.44
	ALL	70.51	9	0.00
3.2.8	imp	chi2	df	Prob
	fi	0.15	1	0.70
	ALL	116.35	9	0.00
3.2.9	tfp	chi2	df	Prob
	fi	5.81	1	0.02
	ALL	60.90	9	0.00
3.2.10	inf	chi2	df	Prob
	fi	0.79	1	0.38
	ALL	56.83	9	0.00

Models

Models		chi2	df	Prob
3.3.4	pcns	chi2	df	Prob
	fm	1.53	1	0.22
	ALL	22.45	9	0.01
3.3.5	inv	chi2	df	Prob
	fm	20.80	1	0.00
	ALL	196.89	9	0.00
3.3.6	gcns	chi2	df	Prob
	fm	0.78	1	0.38
	ALL	74.84	9	0.00
3.3.7	exp	chi2	df	Prob
	fm	7.53	1	0.01
	ALL	108.16	9	0.00
3.3.8	imp	chi2	df	Prob
	fm	29.06	1	0.00
	ALL	181.51	9	0.00
3.3.9	tfp	chi2	df	Prob
	fm	3.80	1	0.05
	ALL	61.23	9	0.00
3.3.10	inf	chi2	df	Prob
	fm	8.56	1	0.00
	ALL	38.10	9	0.00

Notes

Appendix 3.2 can be found at www.routledge.com/9781032372655

1 See Appendix 4 for the Figures of the stability circles.
2 Ensuring the stability condition implies that the panel VAR is invertible and has an infinite-order vector moving-average representations (see Abrigo & Love, 2015).
3 To run empirical models in this book, we have used PVAR in Stata and PVAR programs, proposed by Love and Zicchino (2006) and Abrigo and Love (2015), giving an updated package of programs with additional functionality, including sub-routines to implement Granger (1969) causality tests, and optimal moment and model selection following Andrews and Lu (2001).

References

Abrigo, M. R., and Love, I. 2016. Estimation of panel vector autoregression in stata. *The Stata Journal, 16*(3), 778–804.

Arellano, M., & Bond, S. (1991). Some tests of specification for panel data: Monte Carlo evidence and an application to employment equations. *The Review of Economic Studies*, 58(2), 277–297.

Love, I., & Zicchino, L. (2006). Financial development and dynamic investment behavior: Evidence from panel VAR. *The Quarterly Review of Economics and Finance*, 46(2), 190–210.

Ayadi, R., Arbak, E., Naceur, S. B., and De Groen, W. P. 2015. Determinants of financial development across the mediterranean. In *Economic and social development of the southern and eastern mediterranean countries* (pp. 159–181). Springer, Switzerland.

Ayadi, R., Arbak, E., Naceur, S. B., and De Groen, W. P. (2015). *Determinants of financial development across the mediterranean* (pp. 159–181). Springer International Publishing, Switzerland.

ILO, I., and OECD, W. (2015). Income inequality and labour income share in G20 countries: Trends, Impacts and Causes. Prepared for the G20 Labour and Employment Ministers Meeting and Joint Meeting with the G20 Finance Ministers, Ankara, Turkey, 3–4 September 2015. ILO, Geneva.

Kim, D.-H., and Lin, S.-C. 2010. Dynamic relationship between inflation and financial development. *Macroeconomic Dynamics, 14*(3), 343–364.

Conclusion

The book investigated three major debates on contemporary economies: (i) if the major components of real economic activity (RECs) stimulate aggregate financial development (AFND), financial market development (FMD), and financial organizational development (FOD) but not vice versa; (ii) if RECs and AFND-FOD-FMD jointly suppress compensation of employees (COEs); and (iii) if these two dynamics have incurred any substantial change after the Great Recession of 2008 and 2009.

The book concludes that there was *fundamental, regressive*, and *structural* financialization in the high-income countries (HICs) in the periods 1980–2007 regarding the overall RECs-FND-COEs nexus; fundamental, regressive, and structural financialization in terms of the RECs-FMD-COEs nexus, and regressive financialization regarding the AFND-COEs and the FOD-COEs nexus in the period 1980–2018; and regressive financialization regarding the overall FND-COEs nexus in the period 2008–2018. This conclusion suggests that (i) positive complementarities (PCMTs) between RECs in stimulating AFND, FMD, and FOD, (ii) fragmented or negative effects of AFND, FMD, and FOD on RECs, and (iii) negative complementarities (NCMTs) between RECs and between AFND, FMD, and FOD in de-stimulating COEs demonstrate that there was a systemic mode of governance in creating a finance-driven economic model and that this model depressed real economic performance and labor's share of income in the HICs in the 1980–2007 period. Finance-driven economic governance resulted in the fragmentation of RECs-AFND, RECs-FMD, and RECs-FOD nexuses altogether during the Great Recession and during the ensuing secular stagnation of 2010–2018.

In institutional change terms, this fragmentation can be considered "exhaustion" (Streeck & Thelen, 2005): the *breakdown* (*withering away*) of the orthodox neoclassical mode of governing the RECs-FND nexus. The policy trap between resisting adoption of orthodox Keynesian macroeconomic governance with an egalitarian income policy *and* perpetuating the defunct remnants of the orthodox neoclassical model by quantitative easing instead is a key illustration of this exhaustion. The path-dependence in the FND-COEs nexus is also an outgrowth of the resistance to an egalitarian income policy

DOI: 10.4324/9781003336105-5

in the period 2008–2018. Streeck's question of "*how will capitalism end*" (Streeck, 2016) might be regarded as the global philosophizing of this exhaustion, because the neo-classical theory or its neoliberal practice has yet to give a structural answer of any kind to the so-called policy trap.

In upper-middle-income countries (UMICs), the RECs-FND nexus was managed through a fragmented mode of governance in all three periods: 1980–2007, 2008–2018, and 1980–2018. In other words, there were no macro complementarities (CMTs) in governing the nexus. However, there were *micro financializations* of the fundamental kind, for example, between government expenditures and AFND-FMD, between inward foreign direct investment and AFND-FMD, and between exports and FOD in the 2018 period (micro financialization denotes positive effects running from one or few of RECs to FND but negative or no effect running from FND to those RECs). An interesting theoretical detail for UMICs is the NCMT between investment expenditures and FND. According to some students of financialization, this condition is enough to show financialization (Palley, 2013). However, we suggest that, if the finance sector does not dominate nonfinancial investment, we cannot make a case that there is financialization; financialization denotes finance-driven governance of real economic structures and the existence of negative causation from nonfinancial investment to FND negates this type of domination

In low-middle-income countries (LMICs), there was fundamental financialization regarding RECs-AFND and RECs-FOD nexuses in the period 1980–2018. Given that LMICs are financially less developed than UMICs, this result illustrates that a U-shaped finance-growth relationship does not hold. In other words, financialization is not a linear process in terms of the level of development.

Our findings and definition of financialization support Epstein's thesis that financialization is an economy-wide process that includes international dynamics. However, Epstein's definition, which aligns financialization with the "increasing role" of financial motives, actors, or markets in economic systems, turns out to be ambiguous. Our definition of financialization is based on clear-cut measures that can be substantiated quantitatively (for diverse groups of countries). Unlike Van der Zwan's (2014) definition, our conceptualization of financialization falls short of addressing its political and social dynamics, which turns out to be a key limitation and an essential task for further research.

Out of the findings of this book emerge three niches for further research. First and foremost, financialization should be studied primarily as a macroeconomic issue rather than as a microeconomic or corporate-centered phenomenon, as it revolves primarily around macro CMTs both in HICs and LMICs. It should however be noted that micro financializations, for example, those in UMICs, may evolve into macro financialization through their economy-wide spillover effects. A potential area of research arising out of this option would be to study the complementary dynamics between macro and micro financializations, which might yield to developing policy suggestions to restrain micro financializations before they turn into an overall macro financialization. Second is the study of whether fundamental financialization evolves into regressive financialization or vice versa. Third, the making of financialization analysis by disaggregating financial development into FOD and FMD in order to pinpoint which part of financial system underlies it.

As a corollary, the level of policy formulation (i) should first be macro-oriented rather than micro-oriented, and (ii) should tackle both AFND and its constituents: FOD and FMD. Because, as illustrated, financialization is a system-wide issue that cannot be handled only by "taming" nonfinancial corporations Neo-classical Keynesianism is far from eliminating neither inefficiency-creating nor inequality-creating impact of financialization by focusing only on *its negative effects* on *its creators*, financial or nonfinancial corporations, from a supply-side perspective. Instead of only quantitative easing or low-interest policy, it is necessary first to adopt an egalitarian macro and micro incomes policy by progressive taxation and efficiency-wage regime, respectively, that would both (i) stimulate higher aggregate demand and thus pave the way for the reorganization of RECs in a growth-driven manner and (ii) de-stimulate financialization by restraining the concentration of income in top income groups or socializing idle capital and thereby preventing finance sector from being a growth sector in itself.

References

Palley, T. I. 2013. Financialization: What it is and why it matters. In *Financialization* (pp. 17–40). Springer, New York.

Streeck, W. 2016. *How will capitalism end?: Essays on a failing system.* Verso Books, London.

Streeck, W., and Thelen, K. 2005. *Institutional change in advanced political economies.* Oxford University Press, Oxford.

Van der Zwan, N. 2014. Making sense of financialization. *Socio-Economic Review, 12*(1), 99–129.

Index

Printed in the United States
by Baker & Taylor Publisher Services